African Animals
in ORIGAMI

Other books by John Montroll:

Origami Sculptures

Origami Sea Life by John Montroll and Robert Lang

Origami Inside-Out

Prehistoric Origami *Dinosaurs and Other Creatures*

Animal Origami for the Enthusiast

Origami for the Enthusiast

Easy Origami

African Animals
in ORIGAMI

John Montroll

Dover Publications, Inc.
New York

To Kimmy and Charley

Copyright © 1991 by John Montroll.
All rights reserved under Pan American and International Copyright Conventions.

Published in Canada by General Publishing Company, Ltd., 30 Lesmill Road, Don Mills, Toronto, Ontario.
Published in the United Kingdom by Constable and Company, Ltd., 3 The Lanchesters, 162–164 Fulham Palace Road, London W6 9ER.

This work is first published in 1991 in separate editions by Antroll Publishing Company, Vermont, and Dover Publications, Inc., New York.

Manufactured in the United States of America
Dover Publications, Inc., 31 East 2nd Street, Mineola, N.Y. 11501

Library of Congress Cataloging-in-Publication Data

Montroll, John.
    African animals in origami / John Montroll.
        p.   cm.
    Includes index.
    ISBN 0-486-26977-9
    1. Origami.   2. Animals in art.   I. Title.
TT870.M54   1991
736'.982—dc20
                                    91-37183
                                      CIP

Introduction

Africa is the homeland to some of the most majestic animals. As an origami artist, I wished to compose a collection of those animals. To do so, I created hungry crocodiles, standing flamingos, opened mouth hippos, bushy maned lions, striped zebras, spotted giraffes, and more. It is my hope that you will enjoy creating these animals, too.

The diagrams use the internationally accepted Randlett-Yoshizawa notation along with my own enhancements. The models in this book can be folded from six inch to ten inch square sheets of origami paper, the larger size being best for the complex models. Origami paper can be found in many hobby shops, or purchased from The Friends of The Origami Center of America. For more information about the Friends (books and supplies), send a self-addressed business size envelope with two first class stamps to:

The Friends of The Origami Center of America
15 West, 77th Street
New York, N.Y. 10024

Origami paper can also be ordered through Dover Publications, Inc.:

Dover Publications, Inc.
180 Varick Street
New York, N.Y. 10014

Many people have helped in many ways. The directions have been tested by many origami artists. I wish to thank my friends Greg Domson, Paul Gilden, Joel Orlina, Mike Riggs, and Tamara Trykar-Lu from St. Anselm's Abbey School for their descriptions of African wildlife throughout this book. I especially wish to thank the origami artist Fumiaki Kawahata San for inspiring me to design a striped zebra. Also, I thank my brother Andy Montroll for his help with the production of this book.

John Montroll

Contents

Grass
*
Page 10

Tree
*
Page 11

By the Lakes & Rivers

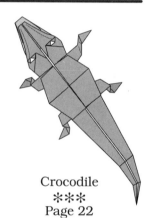

Sacred Ibis
**
Page 14

Crowned Crane
**
Page 16

Flamingo
**
Page 19

Crocodile
***
Page 22

Tropical Rain Forests

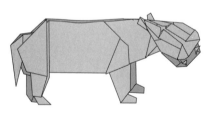
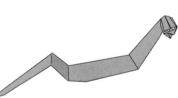
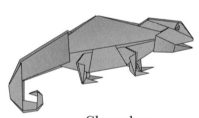

Hipopotamus
***
Page 27

Snake
**
Page 34

Chameleon
**
Page 37

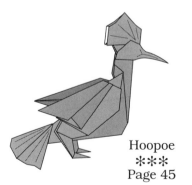

Bee-eater
**
Page 41

Hoopoe
***
Page 45

Hornbill
***
Page 49

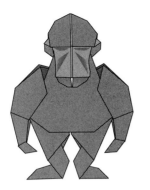

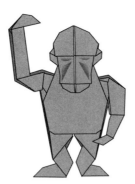

In the Savanna

Symbols

Lines

– – – – – – – – – – Valley fold, fold in front.

– · – · · – · – · – Mountain fold, fold behind.

——————————— Crease line.

· · · · · · · · · · · · · · · · · X-ray or guide line.

Arrows

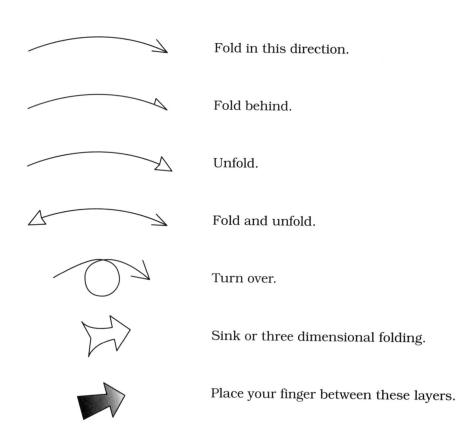

Fold in this direction.

Fold behind.

Unfold.

Fold and unfold.

Turn over.

Sink or three dimensional folding.

Place your finger between these layers.

African Wildlife

Africa has an amazing diverse wildlife population. There are 90 species of hoofed mammals (plus, of course, their attendant predators), 45 species of monkeys, almost 1,500 species of birds, over 2,000 kinds of fish, and uncounted tens of thousands of insect varieties.

Although wildlife roams all over the continent, there are two main areas of concentration, one running south from Ethiopia, the other extending from northwest and north-central Africa down to the Tropic of Cancer. Increasingly in these two areas, wildlife is being concentrated in the great national parks designed to protect the animal populations from the pressures of civilization. Some parks are intended mainly for the large mammals, important both to the ecosystems and to the tourist industry. Other parks, especially in East Africa, have been designed with an eye toward maintaining healthy populations of aquatic and bird life. As the encroachment of man continues, these parks become increasingly important for the survival of the amazing animal array which for many people symbolizes Africa.

Grass

Grasses are the most versatile, widespread, and important of plants. Over 4,000 species of grasses currently exist, from bothersome weeds to the essential rice, wheat, oats, barley, and millet vital to man's survival and to the hundreds of species which provide food and cover to the animals of the African savannas. No origami diorama of African plains animals would be complete without grasses.

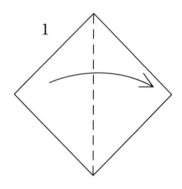

1

2

3

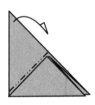

4

Fold behind.

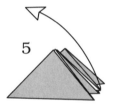

5

Pull out the
middle layer.

6

7

8

Rotate.

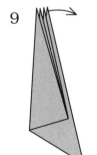

9

Spread the points.

10

11

The grass can stand
on the lower flat part.
Turn over.

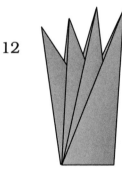

12

Grass

Tree

African trees affect the climate of the rainforests they cover, holding in humidity, keeping light from the forest floor, and moderating temperatures. Some African animals spend their lives in these trees. Others nest there to protect their young from ground-dwelling predators. But these animals and their young sometimes fall prey to other predators, such as snakes, which have adapted themselves for aboreal hunting.

Trees also dot the rich savannas, where elephants keep tree populations in check by knocking the big plants over to get at tender top leaves and shoots. Herds of elephants may even clear small forests, converting a jungle-like environment to a plain.

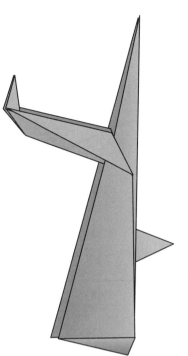

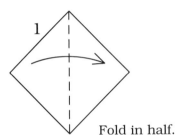

1 Fold in half.

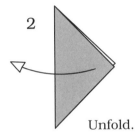

2 Unfold.

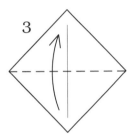

3

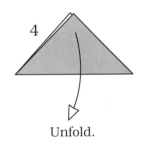

4 Unfold.

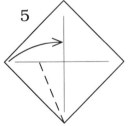

5 Kite-fold but only crease below the center line.

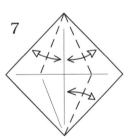

6 Unfold.

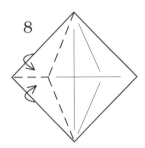

7 Fold and unfold the three other sides.

8

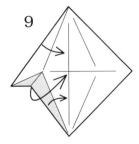

9 A three-dimensional intermediate step.

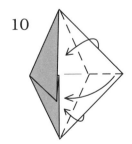

10 A rabbit ear has been completed on the left side. Fold another rabbit ear on the right.

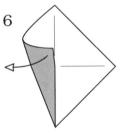

11

12

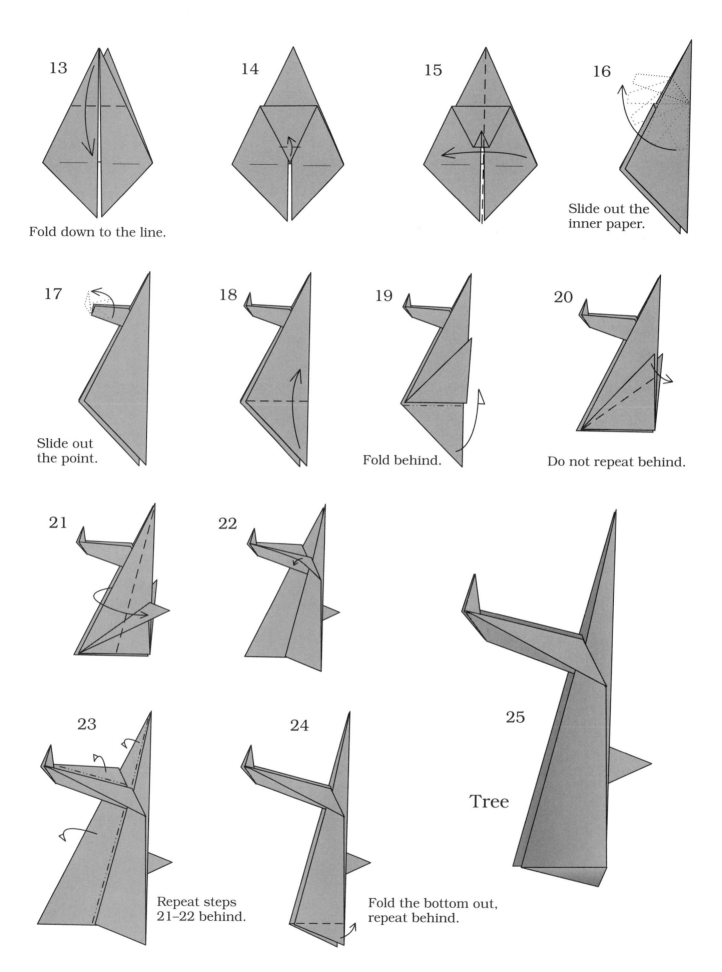

13 Fold down to the line.

14

15

16 Slide out the inner paper.

17 Slide out the point.

18

19 Fold behind.

20 Do not repeat behind.

21

22

23 Repeat steps 21–22 behind.

24 Fold the bottom out, repeat behind.

25 Tree

By the Lakes & Rivers

The African continent is pockmarked with enormous lakes. Many of these lie along the Great Rift, the geological crack that runs down Africa's eastern spine. From two big lakes flows the Nile, which carries water from the rainy heart of Africa to the parched northeastern quadrant. Its legendary source by the Mountains of the Moon was the object of more than a millenium of searches by European explorers. Further south, other large rivers—most notably the Zaire and the Zambezi—bring water to the Indian and Atlantic oceans and provide a home for tens of millions of birds, reptiles, and mammals.

Sacred Ibis

The ibis belongs to the stork family. It has a slim curved beak and few feathers on the throat or face. Like storks, ibises extend their necks forward in flight; groups of ibises fly in V-formation. The sacred ibis was revered in ancient Egypt, as long as 5000 years ago. It was considered the embodiment of Thoth, the god of wisdom, and the scribe of the gods. He was shown in sculptures and paintings as a human with an ibis-head, who gave the hieroglyph of life to Osiris. The ibis was also a hieroglyphic symbol. Since it was sacred, it was often mummified after death; whole cemeteries of well-preserved ibis mummies have been discovered in Egypt. Farther south, they are a common sight on African lakes and rivers.

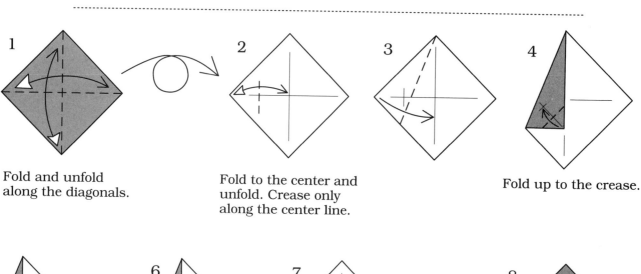

1

Fold and unfold along the diagonals.

2

Fold to the center and unfold. Crease only along the center line.

3

4

Fold up to the crease.

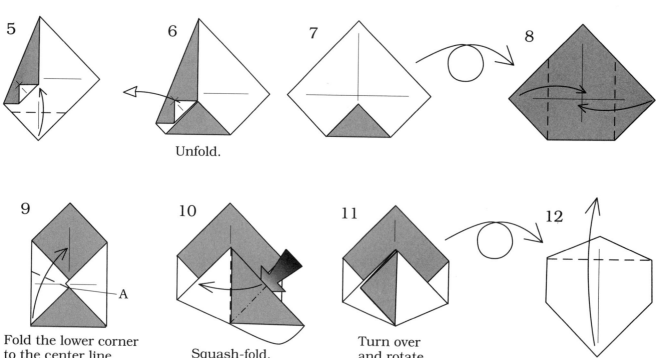

5

6

Unfold.

7

8

9

Fold the lower corner to the center line using A as a guide.

10

Squash-fold.

11

Turn over and rotate.

12

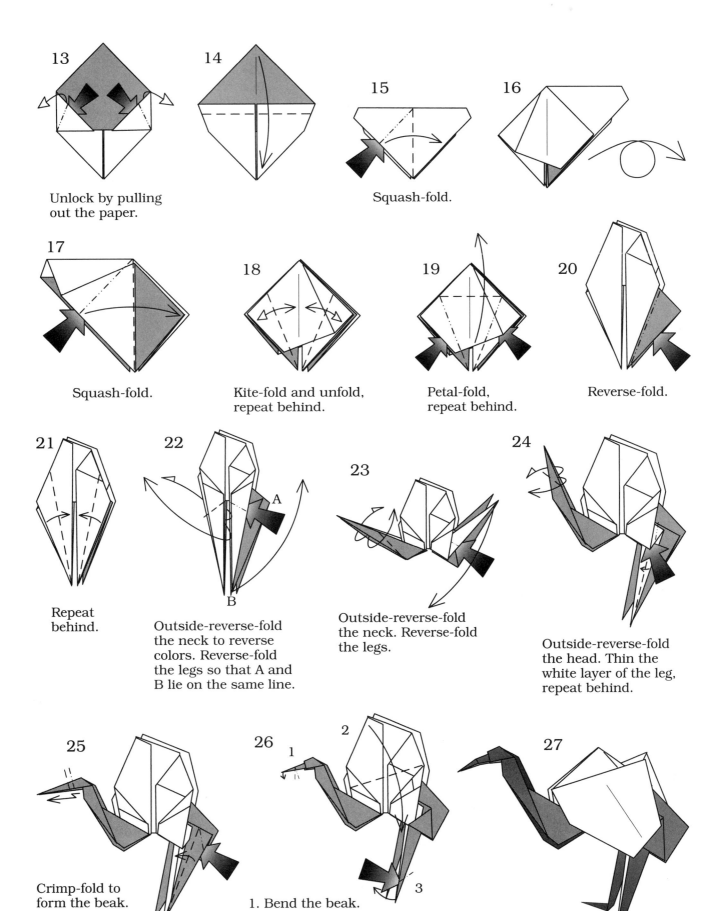

13

Unlock by pulling out the paper.

14

15

Squash-fold.

16

17

Squash-fold.

18

Kite-fold and unfold, repeat behind.

19

Petal-fold, repeat behind.

20

Reverse-fold.

21

Repeat behind.

22

A

B

Outside-reverse-fold the neck to reverse colors. Reverse-fold the legs so that A and B lie on the same line.

23

Outside-reverse-fold the neck. Reverse-fold the legs.

24

Outside-reverse-fold the head. Thin the white layer of the leg, repeat behind.

25

Crimp-fold to form the beak. Squash-fold to thin the leg, repeat behind.

26

1

2

3

1. Bend the beak.
2. Fold the wings down.
3. Reverse-fold the feet and adjust them so the ibis can stand.

27

Sacred Ibis

Crowned Crane

Crowned cranes are colorful and named for the crown of straight, thin, white feathers on the back of their heads. They live in open landscapes and occasionally build their nests in trees. There are several sub-species. Black-necked cranes are popular in West Africa and are raised there as domestic animals. The grey-necked crane of South and Southeast Africa has a unique method of hunting for locusts. It stamps both feet repeatedly on the ground, thereby scaring the insects and causing them to fly up. Then the crane can devour them at leisure.

1

Fold and unfold.

2

3

Fold and unfold, repeat behind.

4

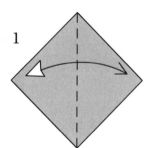

5

Unfold.

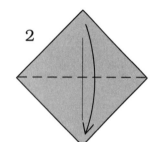

6

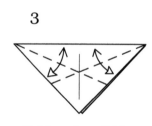

7

Fold corner A to line B–C starting at D.

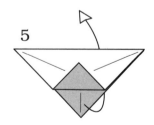

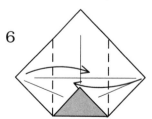

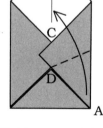

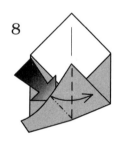

8

Squash-fold.

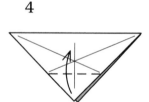

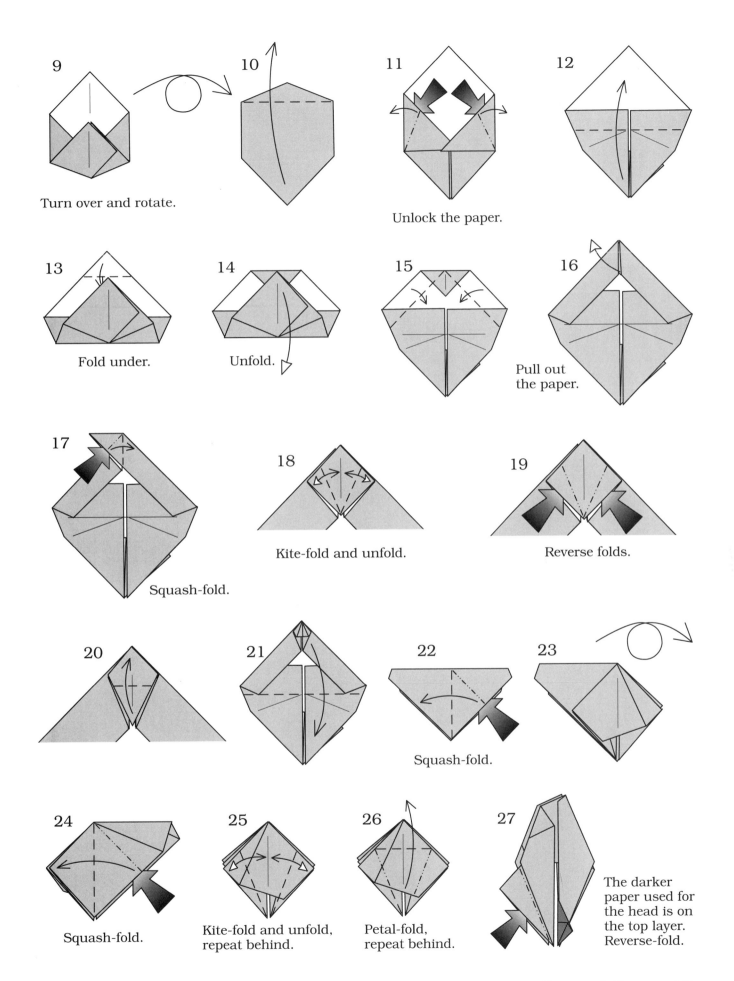

9

Turn over and rotate.

10

11

Unlock the paper.

12

13

Fold under.

14

Unfold.

15

16

Pull out
the paper.

17

Squash-fold.

18

Kite-fold and unfold.

19

Reverse folds.

20

21

22

Squash-fold.

23

24

Squash-fold.

25

Kite-fold and unfold,
repeat behind.

26

Petal-fold,
repeat behind.

27

The darker
paper used for
the head is on
the top layer.
Reverse-fold.

Crowned Crane 17

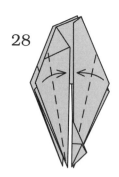

28

Repeat behind.

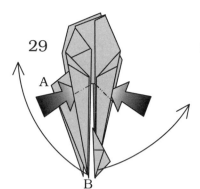

29

A

B

Reverse-fold the neck.
Reverse-fold the legs
so that A and B lie on
the same line.

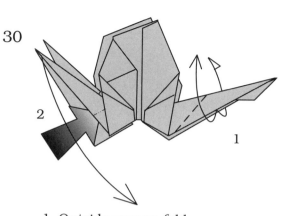

30

2

1

1. Outside-reverse-fold.
2. Reverse-fold, repeat behind.

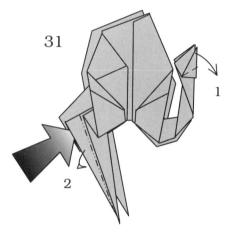

31

1

2

1. Outside-reverse-fold.
2. Thin the leg, repeat behind.

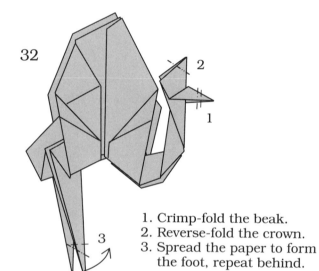

32

2

1

3

1. Crimp-fold the beak.
2. Reverse-fold the crown.
3. Spread the paper to form
   the foot, repeat behind.

33

Spread the wings and puff
out the body. Adjust the
feet so the crane can stand.

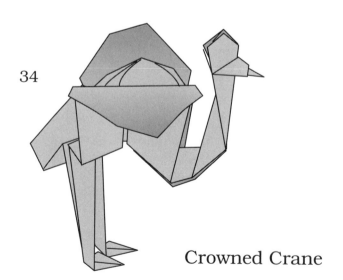

34

Crowned Crane

Flamingo

Flamingos are water birds with extremely long legs and long, curved necks with 19 vertebrae. When they sift for food in the water, they hold their beaks upside down. They live in large flocks of up to several hundred thousand birds, in salt lakes, coastal waters, and lagoons. In the wilds of Africa flamingos are a rich pink, but they maintain this characteristic color in captivity only if they are fed red carotene pills.

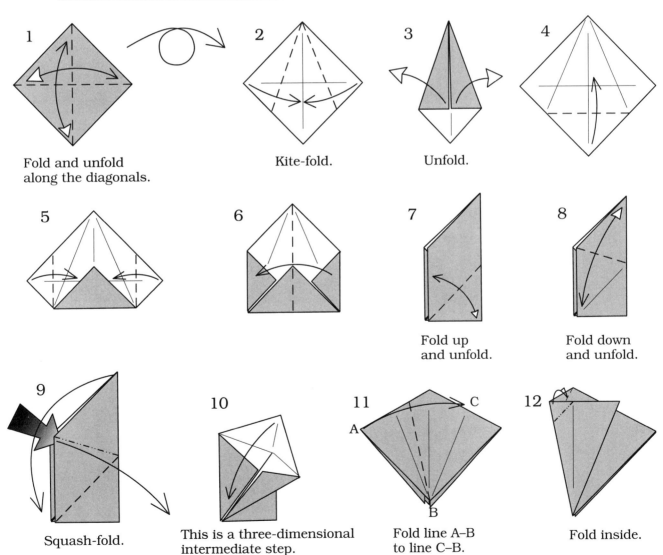

1 Fold and unfold along the diagonals.

2 Kite-fold.

3 Unfold.

4

5

6

7 Fold up and unfold.

8 Fold down and unfold.

9 Squash-fold.

10 This is a three-dimensional intermediate step.

11 Fold line A–B to line C–B.

12 Fold inside.

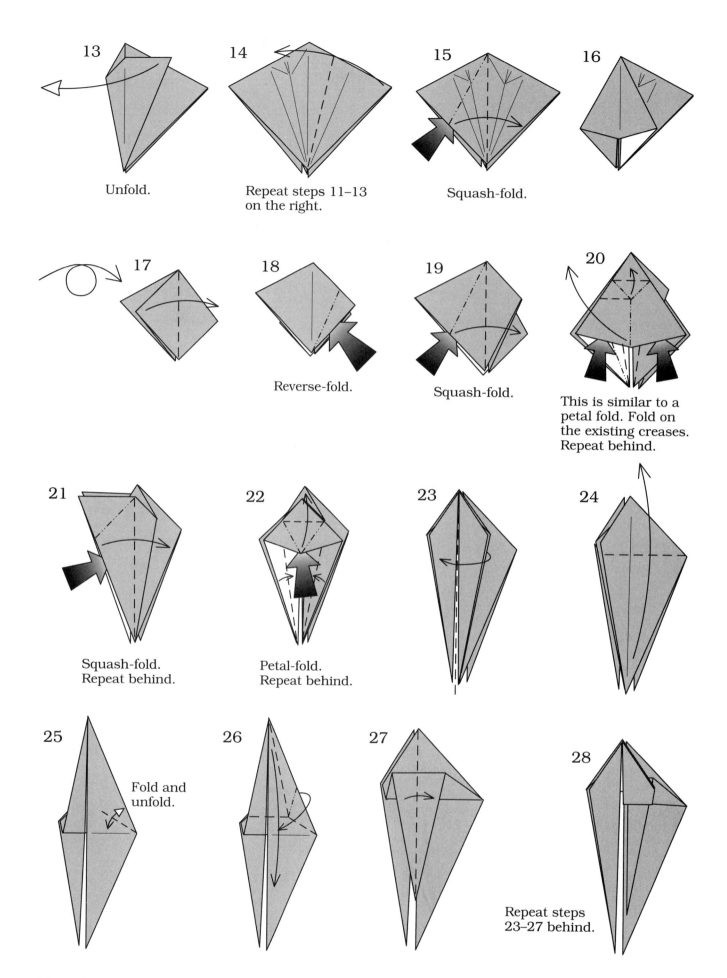

13

Unfold.

14

Repeat steps 11–13
on the right.

15

Squash-fold.

16

17

18

Reverse-fold.

19

Squash-fold.

20

This is similar to a
petal fold. Fold on
the existing creases.
Repeat behind.

21

Squash-fold.
Repeat behind.

22

Petal-fold.
Repeat behind.

23

24

25

Fold and
unfold.

26

27

28

Repeat steps
23–27 behind.

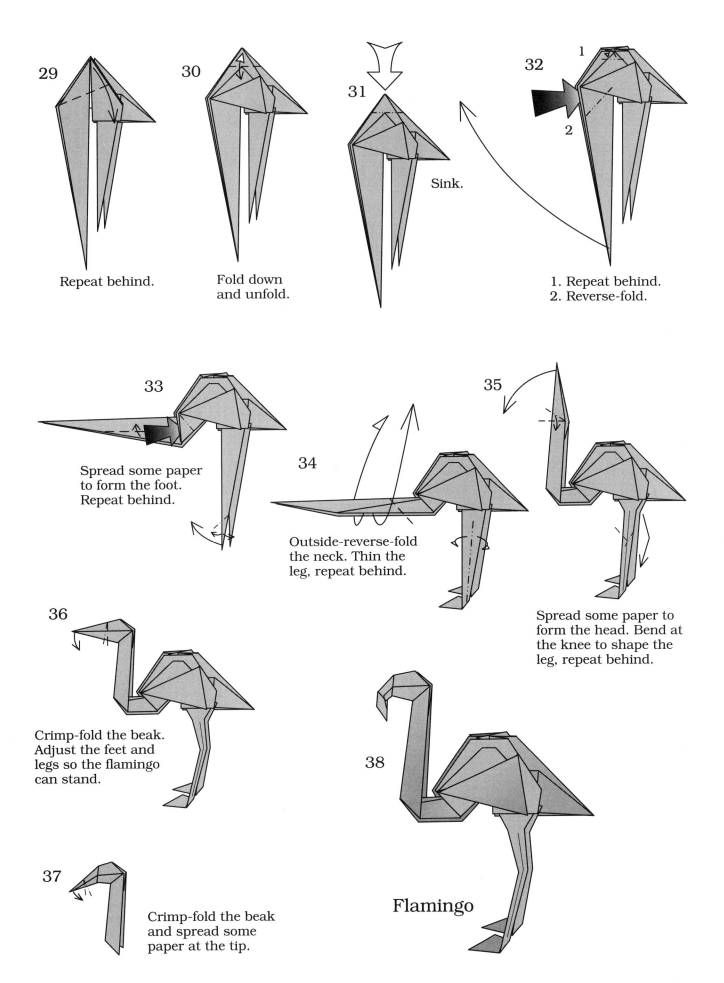

29

Repeat behind.

30

Fold down
and unfold.

31

Sink.

32

1
2

1. Repeat behind.
2. Reverse-fold.

33

Spread some paper
to form the foot.
Repeat behind.

34

Outside-reverse-fold
the neck. Thin the
leg, repeat behind.

35

Spread some paper to
form the head. Bend at
the knee to shape the
leg, repeat behind.

36

Crimp-fold the beak.
Adjust the feet and
legs so the flamingo
can stand.

37

Crimp-fold the beak
and spread some
paper at the tip.

38

Flamingo

Crocodile

The crocodile is one of the largest living reptiles. It has a low, sleek, cigarette-shaped body, short legs, and a powerful tail which aids it in swimming. Crocodiles are smaller than their cousins, the alligators, and have a pointier snout.

Crocodiles inhabit tropical areas worldwide, preferring such locales as sluggish rivers, open swamps, and marshes. Their webbed feet enable them to tread on soft ground while their well-placed eyes and nostrils allow them to skim the water with only their eyes and nostrils above the surface. Crocodiles prey on fish, birds, small mammals, and occasionally on larger mammals, including people. They are a dangerous resident and ecologically important predator in rivers throughout Africa.

> "How doth the little crocodile
> Improve his shining tail,
> And pour the waters of the Nile
> On every golden scale.
>
> "How cheerfully he seems to grin,
> How neatly spreads his claws,
> And welcomes little fishes in,
> With gently snapping jaws!"

—Lewis Carroll

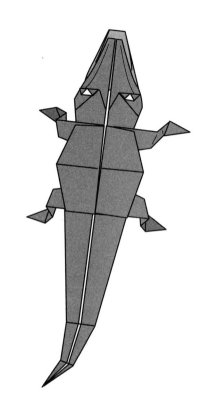

1

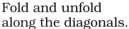

Fold and unfold
along the diagonals.

2

Kite-fold.

3

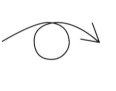

Unfold.

4

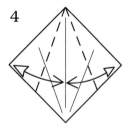

Fold and unfold.

5

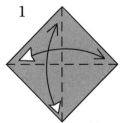

6

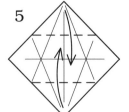

Fold in half and unfold.

7

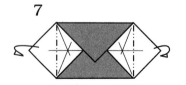

8

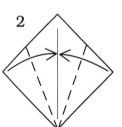

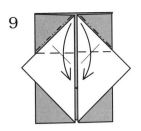

9

Squash folds. Note
that the crease lines
are on the top.

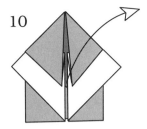

10

Pull out the inside,
darker paper.

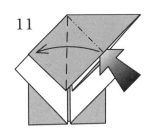

11

Squash-fold.

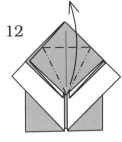

12

Petal-fold.

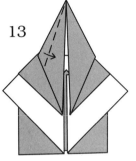

13

Fold at an angle
of slightly less
than one-third.

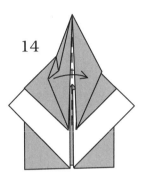

14

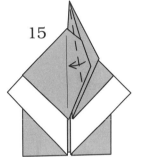

15

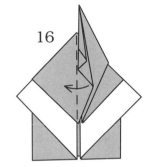

16

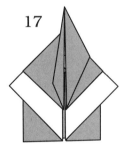

17

Repeat steps 13–16 on
the right and rotate.

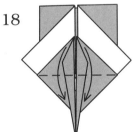

18

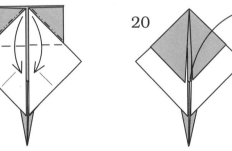

19

Squash-fold.

20

Pull out the corner.

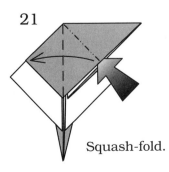

21

Squash-fold.

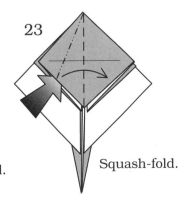

22

Fold up
and unfold.

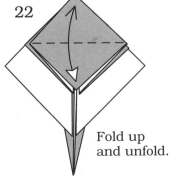

23

Squash-fold.

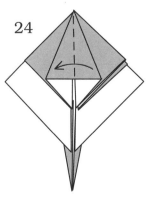

24

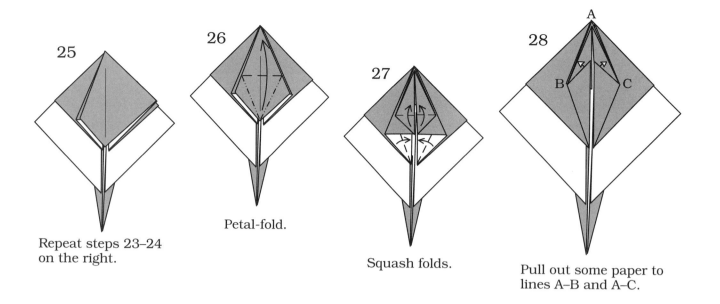

25

Repeat steps 23–24
on the right.

26

Petal-fold.

27

Squash folds.

28

A

B   C

Pull out some paper to
lines A–B and A–C.

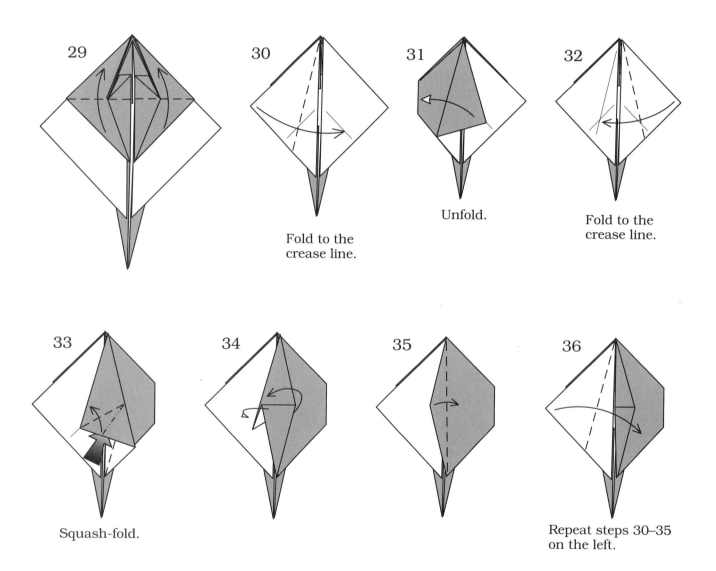

29

30

Fold to the
crease line.

31

Unfold.

32

Fold to the
crease line.

33

Squash-fold.

34

35

36

Repeat steps 30–35
on the left.

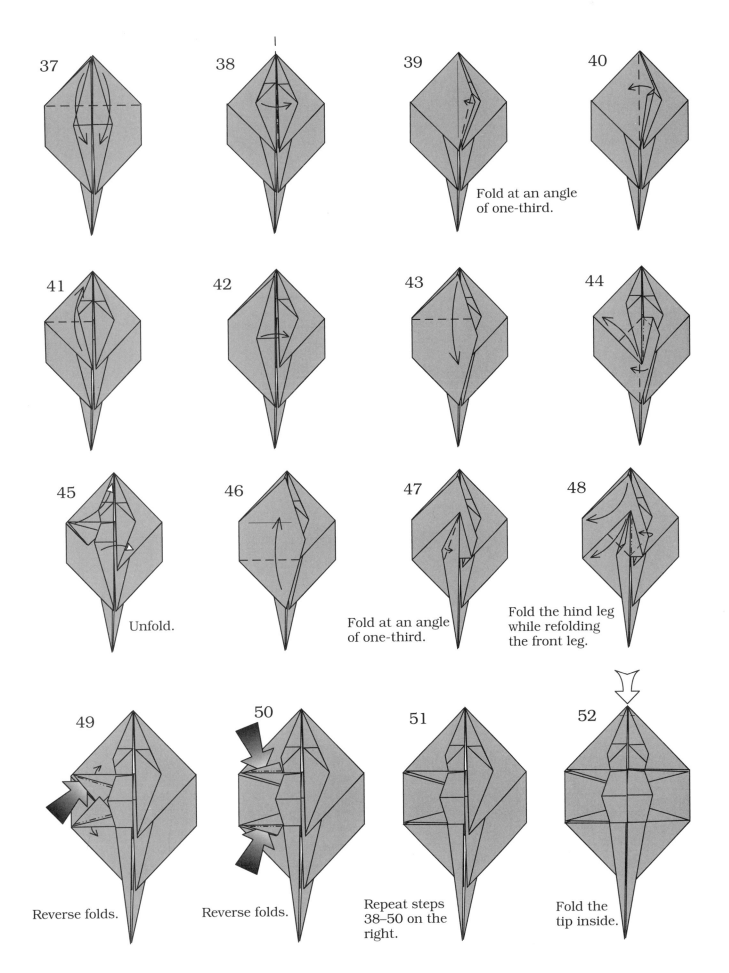

37

38

39
Fold at an angle of one-third.

40

41

42

43

44

45
Unfold.

46

47
Fold at an angle of one-third.

48
Fold the hind leg while refolding the front leg.

49
Reverse folds.

50
Reverse folds.

51
Repeat steps 38–50 on the right.

52
Fold the tip inside.

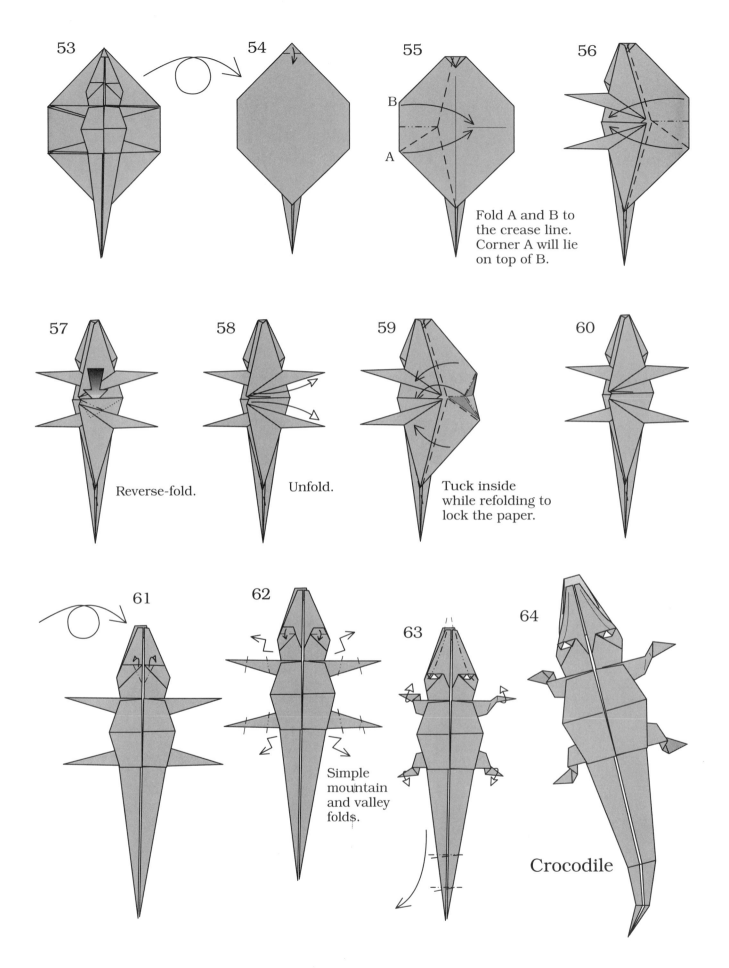

53

54

55

B

A

Fold A and B to
the crease line.
Corner A will lie
on top of B.

56

57

Reverse-fold.

58

Unfold.

59

Tuck inside
while refolding to
lock the paper.

60

61

62

Simple
mountain
and valley
folds.

63

64

Crocodile

Hippopotamus

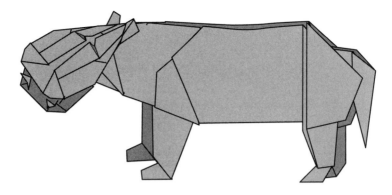

The name "hippopotamus" comes from the Greek and means "river horse". The plural is "hippopotamuses". There are two species of this animal, a pygmy which lives in forests, and a larger one in grasslands. The large species can grow 10 feet long, four feet high, and weigh up to 7000 pounds. The hippo has different daytime and nighttime activities and habitats. Since its skin structure causes high fluid condensation in the air, it has to live in the water during the day. Its head is well adapted to aquatic life: eyes, ears, and nostrils are situated at the top. It can stay submerged under water for up to five minutes, and it need only lift its head to breathe. During the night the hippo feeds on vegetation—roots, grasses, fruits. The hippopotamus eats little in relation to its body weight, probably because it does not expend much energy in moving about and spends a lot of time resting. It can open its jaws to a 150 degree angle, and it does so mostly to yawn.

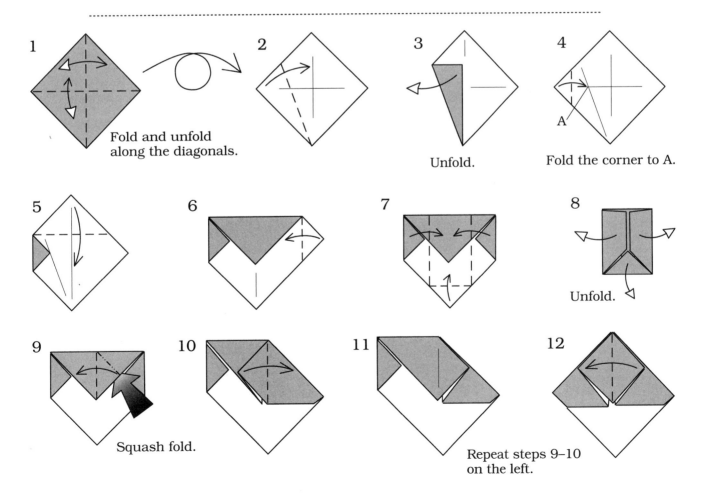

1 Fold and unfold along the diagonals.

2

3 Unfold.

4 Fold the corner to A.

5

6

7

8 Unfold.

9 Squash fold.

10

11 Repeat steps 9–10 on the left.

12

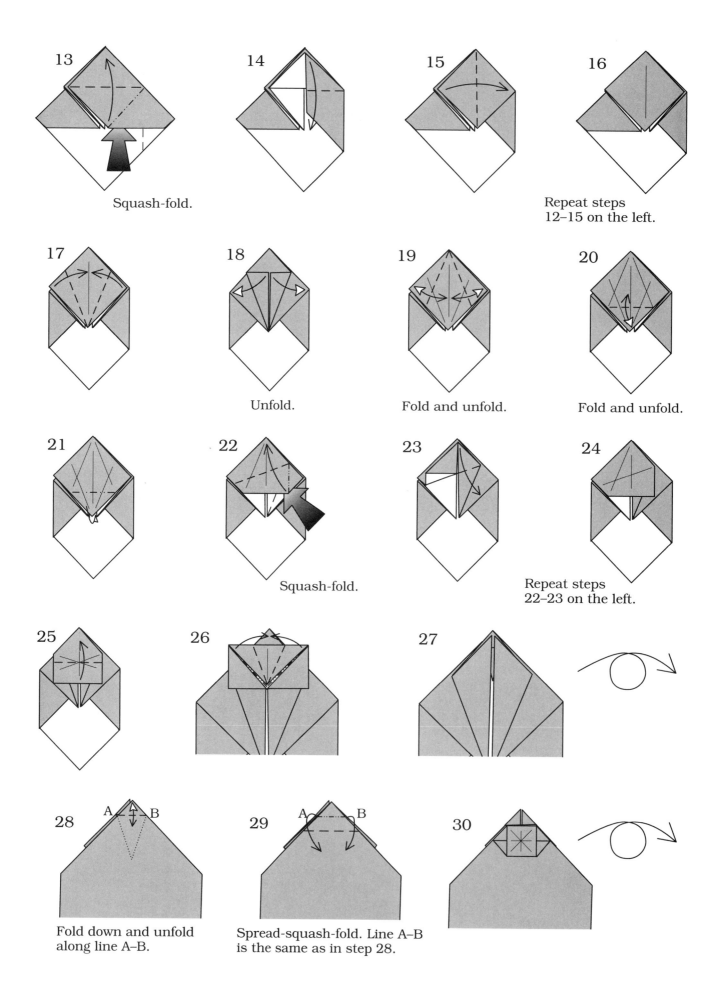

13

Squash-fold.

14

15

16

Repeat steps
12–15 on the left.

17

18

Unfold.

19

Fold and unfold.

20

Fold and unfold.

21

22

Squash-fold.

23

24

Repeat steps
22–23 on the left.

25

26

27

28

A B

Fold down and unfold
along line A–B.

29

A B

Spread-squash-fold. Line A–B
is the same as in step 28.

30

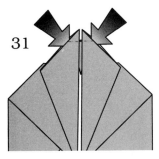

31

Reverse folds.

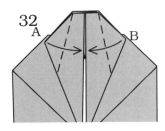

32

A B

Fold corners A and B to the center.

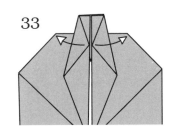

33

Unfold.

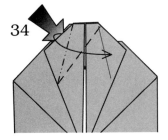

34

Spread-squash-fold.

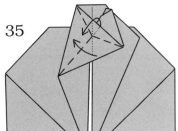

35

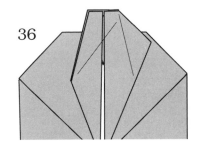

36

Repeat steps 34–35 on the right.

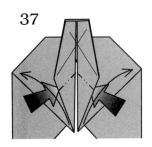

37

Reverse folds.

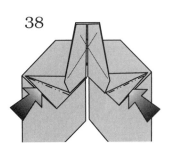

38

Reverse folds.

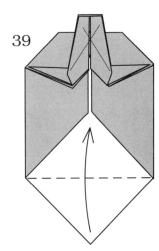

39

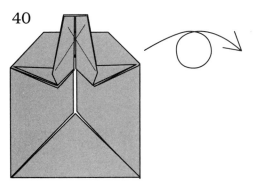

40

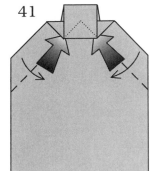

41

Reverse folds.

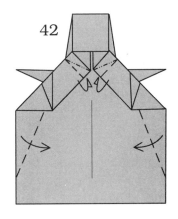

42

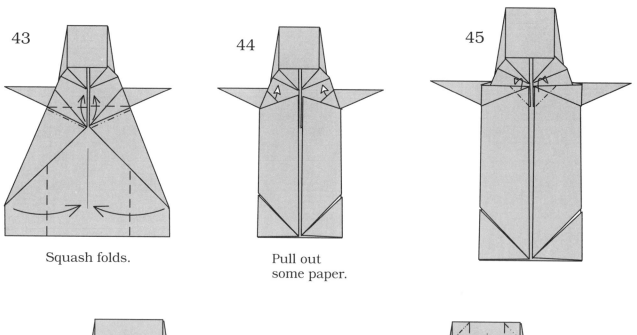

43 Squash folds.

44 Pull out some paper.

45

46 For these reverse folds, tuck the paper into the lower layers.

47 Spread-squash folds.

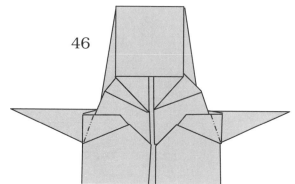

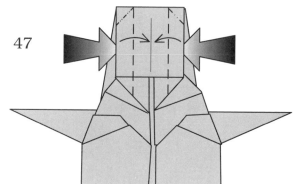

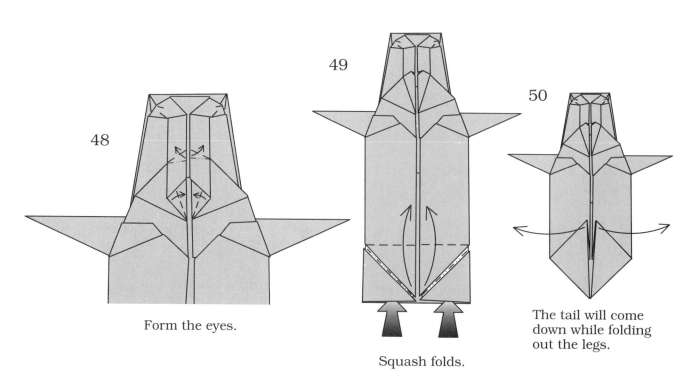

48 Form the eyes.

49 Squash folds.

50 The tail will come down while folding out the legs.

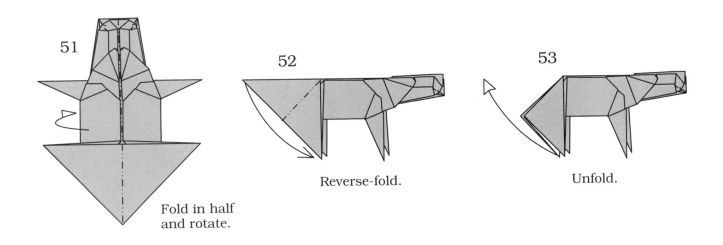

51

Fold in half
and rotate.

52

Reverse-fold.

53

Unfold.

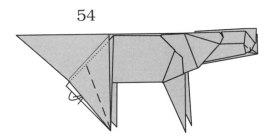

54

Fold the inner layers.
Repeat behind.

55

Reverse-fold.

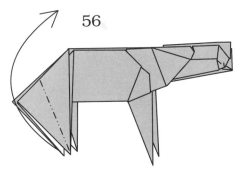

56

Petal-fold the tail up.

57

Reverse-fold.

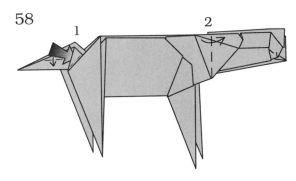

58

1

2

Repeat behind at the tail and ear.

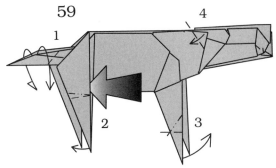

59

1

4

2

3

1. Outside-reverse-fold.
2. Crimp-fold the knee, repeat behind.
3. Crimp-fold the foot, repeat behind.
4. Repeat behind.

Hippopotamus 31

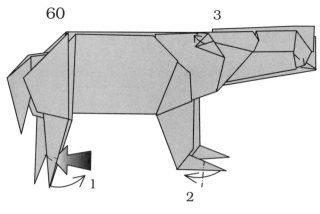

60

3

1

2

1. Shape the foot.
2. Reverse-fold.
3. Pull out some paper
   by the ear.
Repeat behind.

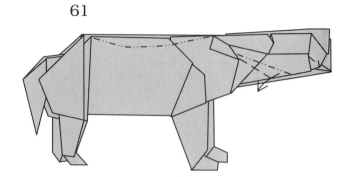

61

Flatten the head, open the
mouth, and shape the back.
Repeat behind.

62

This is a front
view of the head.

63

This is a view of the
jaw. Rabbit-ear to
form two teeth.

64

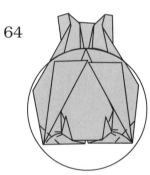

Tuck the corners
under the teeth.

65

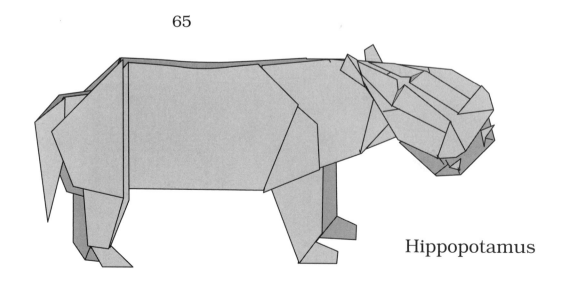

Hippopotamus

Tropical Rain Forests

Generally speaking, the tropical rain forest is a forest of tall trees found on or near the Equator and characterized by consistently high temperatures and abundant rainfall throughout the year. These weather conditions create a climatic region bursting with beauty and life. The jungles and tropical rain forests of Africa are no exception: they are the home of some of Africa's most fascinating creatures.

The weather in a tropical rain forest does not undergo much change throughout the year. The temperature rarely tops 93° F or drops below 68° F. In fact, average temperatures in the hottest month may be separated from average temperatures in the coldest month by only 2° to 5° F. Yearly rainfall in a tropical rain forest is obviously heavy, with averages between 60 and 140 inches. The combination of high heat and moisture also makes conditions humid and cloudy at virtually all times.

A tropical rain forest has more species of plants and animals than any other region in the world. An 8-acre rain forest may contain 180 species of trees. Moreover, there are more of certain species of animals—amphibians, birds, insects, mammals, and reptiles—housed by tropical rain forests than by any other area in the world.

Tropical rain forests cover less than a fifth of Africa in total surface area. The most prominent rain forests, where distinctive broad-leaf evergreen trees grow, are found in the Congo River Basin, southern Nigeria, and other coastal areas of West Africa. There are tropical forests in the highlands of Ethiopia and even among the mountains of northwestern Africa. Finally, open forests grow on the plateaus of south-central Africa, south of the Congo River Basin.

Animal life in the rain forests is highly adapted to the plant growth. Because the tallest trees in the forest form a canopy 100 to 180 feet above the ground, many inhabitants of the forest spend all their lives in the trees and rarely descend to the ground. Examples of these are birds, bats, monkeys, squirrels, and parrots. Assorted frogs and lizards also dwell among the trees. Most of these animals are well-suited to treetop life. Many animals also roam on or slightly above the forest floor. Bees, mosquitoes, and spiders are often joined by antelope, hogs, and various rodents. There are also chimpanzees, gorillas, and several members of the cat family that live both on the floor and in the trees.

Snake

The snake is a reptile with a long legless body covered with dry scales. Despite the generalized description, snakes have many unusual body features and fascinating ways of life. To move on land, a snake usually slides on its belly. Many snakes have a flexible body that can coil into a ball. The eyes of a snake are covered by clear scales instead of movable eyelids. Therefore, snake eyes are always open. Snakes have a narrow, forked tongue which they repeatedly flick in and out. This brings odors to a special organ in their mouth which allows them to follow the scent trails of their prey.

Snakes are found almost everywhere on earth. They inhabit deserts, forests, oceans, streams, and lakes. Many snakes live above ground in trees, on the ground, underground, or in the water. Only a few areas in the world have no snakes. There are no snakes where the ground stays frozen year round. Being cold-blooded, snakes would not survive there—thus there are no snakes in the polar regions or at high elevations in the mountains. There are also no snakes in Ireland or New Zealand.

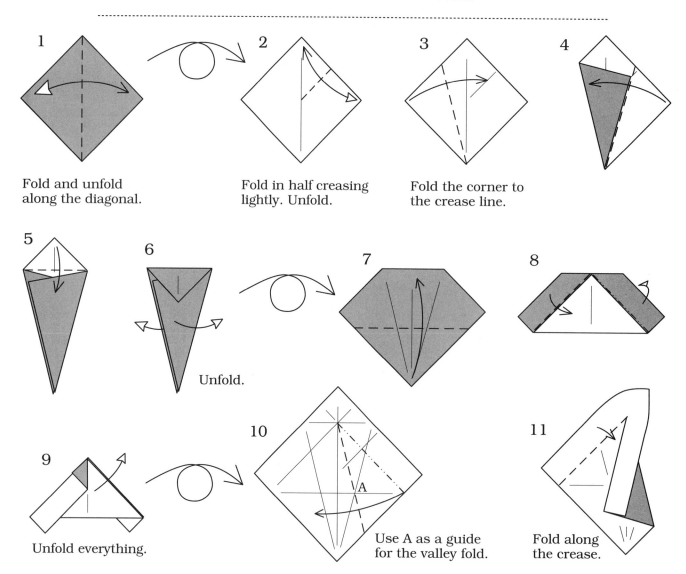

1 Fold and unfold along the diagonal.

2 Fold in half creasing lightly. Unfold.

3 Fold the corner to the crease line.

4

5

6 Unfold.

7

8

9 Unfold everything.

10 Use A as a guide for the valley fold.

11 Fold along the crease.

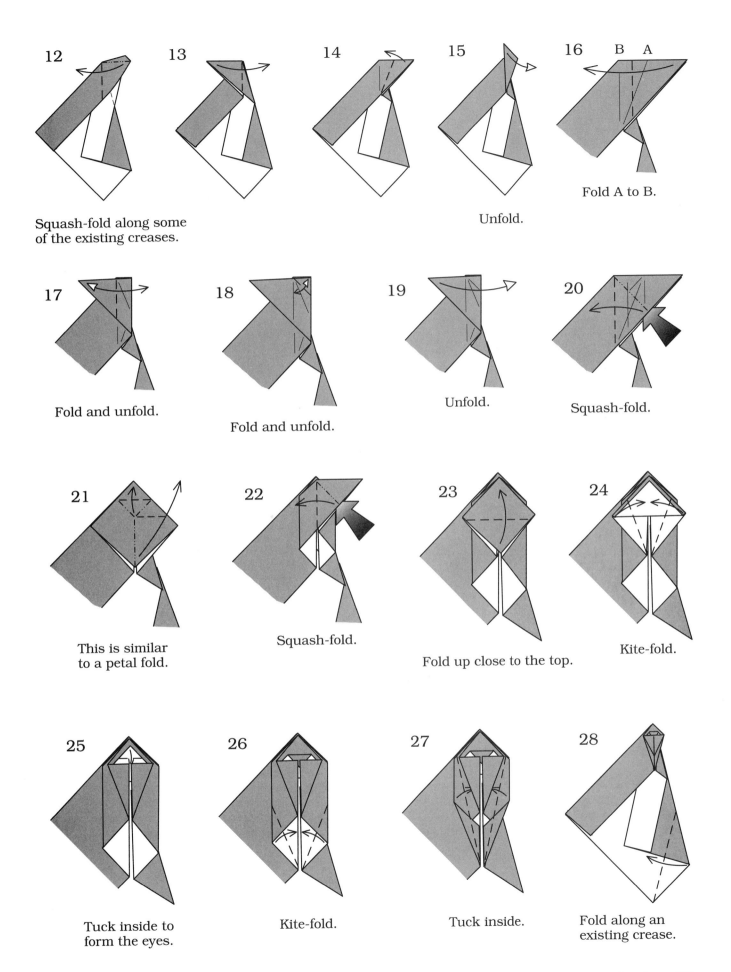

12 Squash-fold along some of the existing creases.

13

14

15 Unfold.

16 B A

Fold A to B.

17 Fold and unfold.

18 Fold and unfold.

19 Unfold.

20 Squash-fold.

21 This is similar to a petal fold.

22 Squash-fold.

23 Fold up close to the top.

24 Kite-fold.

25 Tuck inside to form the eyes.

26 Kite-fold.

27 Tuck inside.

28 Fold along an existing crease.

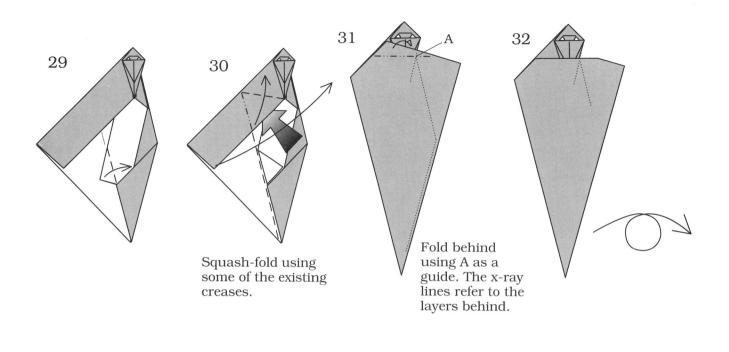

29

30 Squash-fold using some of the existing creases.

31 A Fold behind using A as a guide. The x-ray lines refer to the layers behind.

32

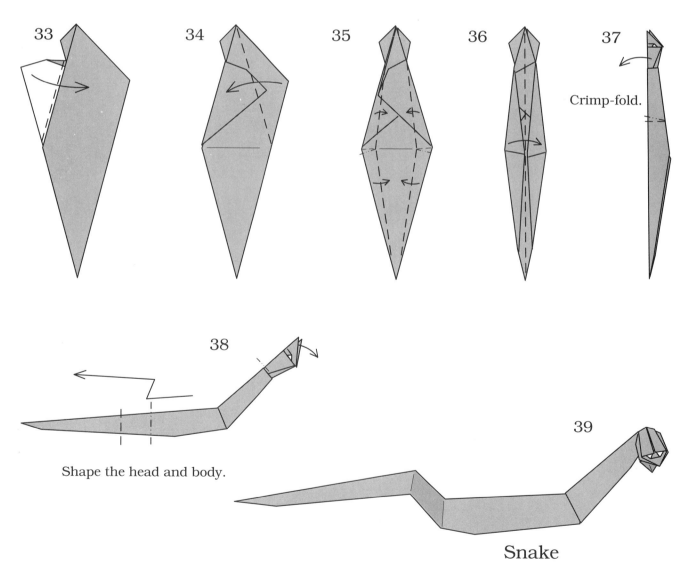

33

34

35

36

37 Crimp-fold.

38 Shape the head and body.

39

Snake

Chameleon

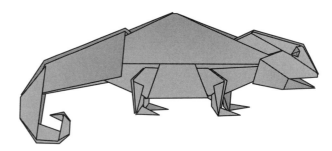

The chameleon is a lizard native to the rain forests of Africa and Madagascar. Some have been found as far as Southern Asia and Europe. There are over 100 different kinds of chameleons.

Among the chameleon's distinguishing features are its slim profile, bulging eyes, and grasping tail. The chameleon's body is flat from side to side, looking as if it had been mashed out of shape. The chameleon's eyes have the unique ability to roll about separately. Therefore the chameleon may view a twig on its left and a crawling insect on its right. Unlike other lizards, the chameleon uses its tail and its feet to grasp the twig or branch supporting it. When not in use the tail curls into a spiral behind the chameleon.

As a slow moving lizard, the chameleon feeds by snaring insects with its tongue. The chameleon's tongue is as long as its body, ends in a sticky knoblike tip, and is controlled by the chameleon's powerful throat muscles. Chameleons also have the ability to change their skin color in response to changes in temperature, light, and emotion. This ability has given us the term "chameleon" to describe any skill in imitation or disguise.

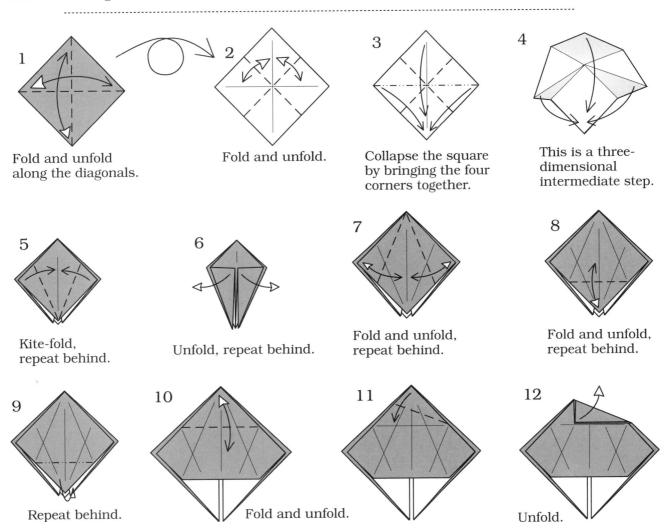

1. Fold and unfold along the diagonals.

2. Fold and unfold.

3. Collapse the square by bringing the four corners together.

4. This is a three-dimensional intermediate step.

5. Kite-fold, repeat behind.

6. Unfold, repeat behind.

7. Fold and unfold, repeat behind.

8. Fold and unfold, repeat behind.

9. Repeat behind.

10. Fold and unfold.

11.

12. Unfold.

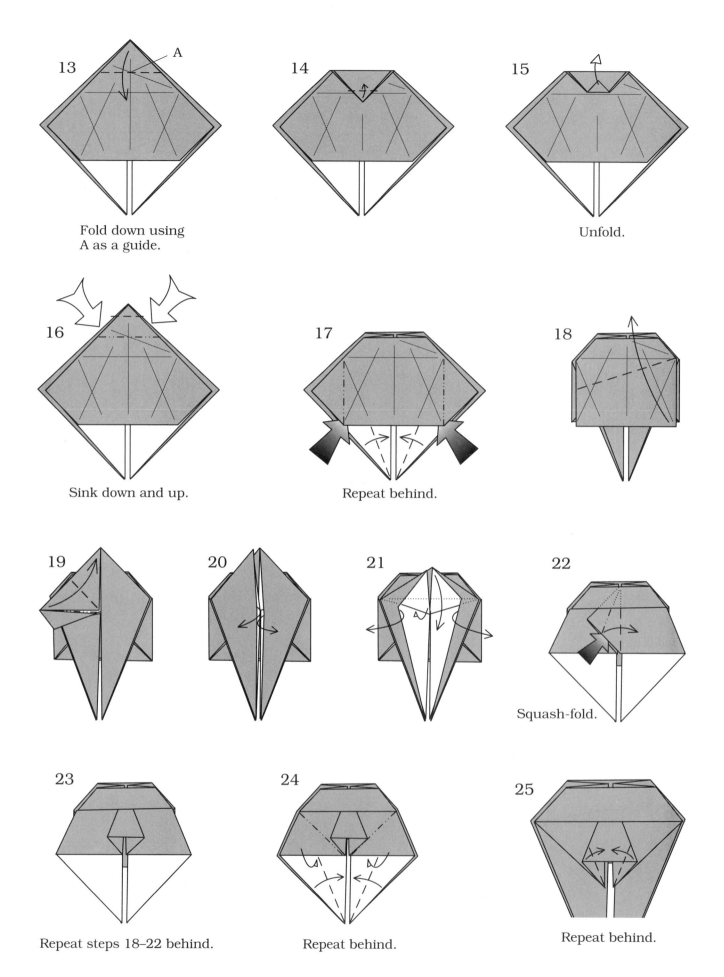

13

A

Fold down using
A as a guide.

14

15

Unfold.

16

Sink down and up.

17

Repeat behind.

18

19

20

21

22

Squash-fold.

23

Repeat steps 18–22 behind.

24

Repeat behind.

25

Repeat behind.

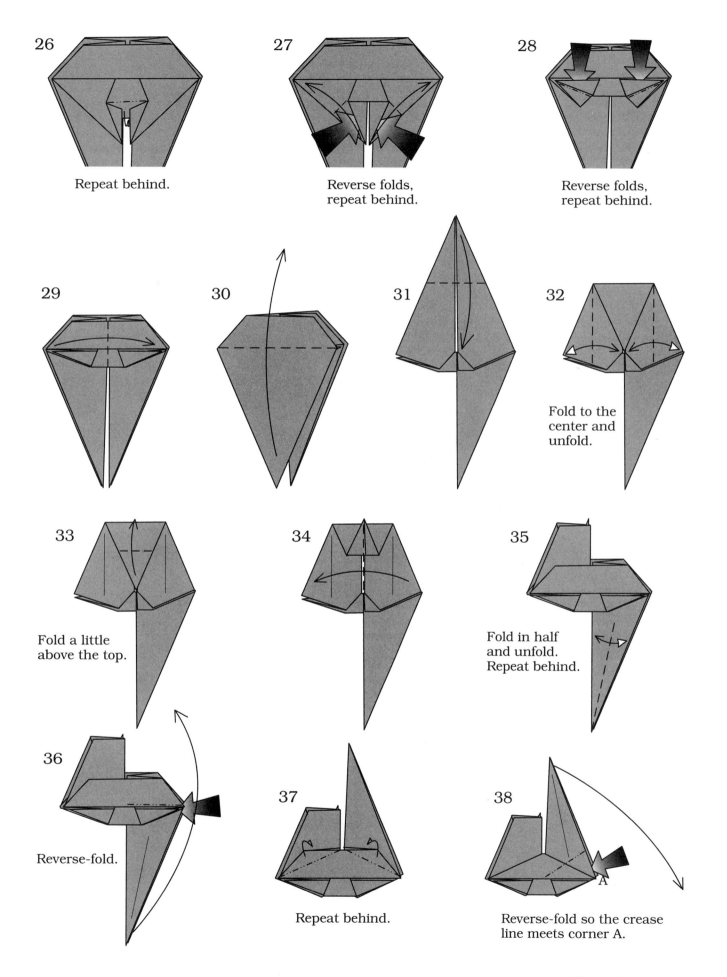

26

Repeat behind.

27

Reverse folds,
repeat behind.

28

Reverse folds,
repeat behind.

29

30

31

32

Fold to the
center and
unfold.

33

Fold a little
above the top.

34

35

Fold in half
and unfold.
Repeat behind.

36

Reverse-fold.

37

Repeat behind.

38

A

Reverse-fold so the crease
line meets corner A.

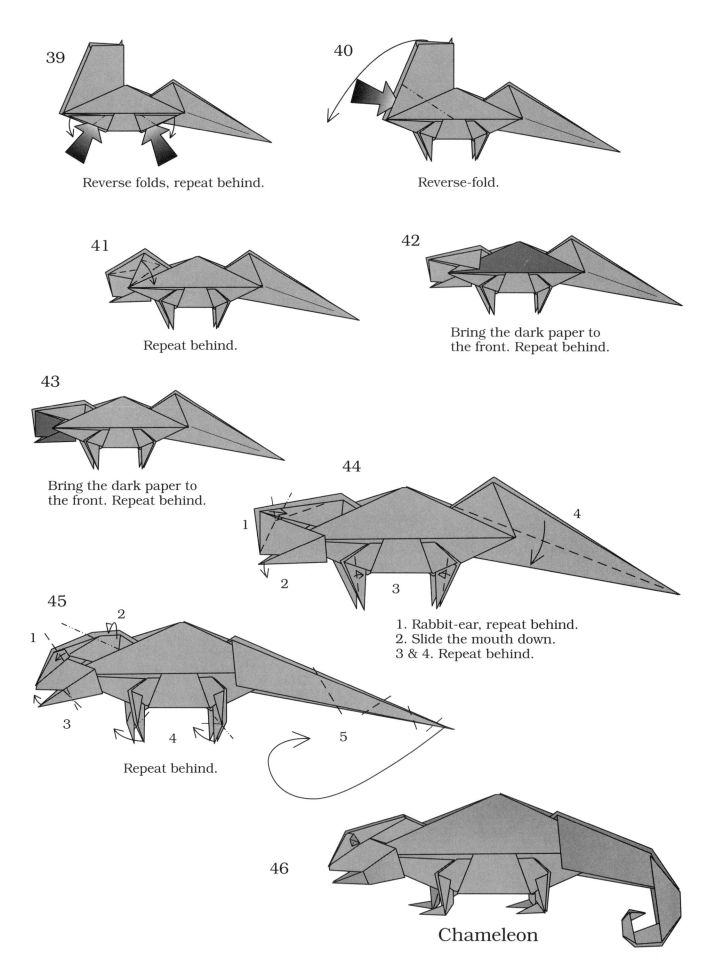

39

Reverse folds, repeat behind.

40

Reverse-fold.

41

Repeat behind.

42

Bring the dark paper to the front. Repeat behind.

43

Bring the dark paper to the front. Repeat behind.

44

1
2
3
4

1. Rabbit-ear, repeat behind.
2. Slide the mouth down.
3 & 4. Repeat behind.

45

1
2
3
4
5

Repeat behind.

46

Chameleon

Bee-eater

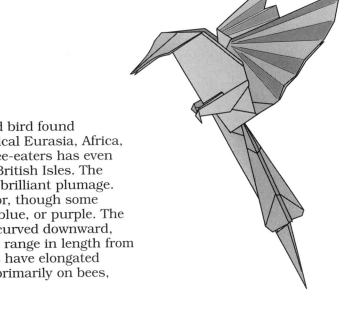

The bee-eater is a highly-colored bird found throughout tropical and subtropical Eurasia, Africa, and Australia. One species of bee-eaters has even been found as far north as the British Isles. The bee-eater is chiefly noted for its brilliant plumage. Bright green is a prominent color, though some species are colored red, yellow, blue, or purple. The bill is moderately long, slightly curved downward, and sharply pointed. Bee-eaters range in length from 6 to 14 inches. Many bee-eaters have elongated central tail feathers. They feed primarily on bees, wasps, and other insects.

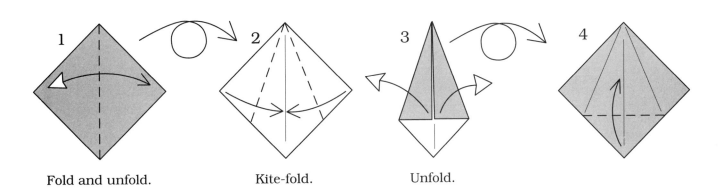

1 Fold and unfold.

2 Kite-fold.

3 Unfold.

4

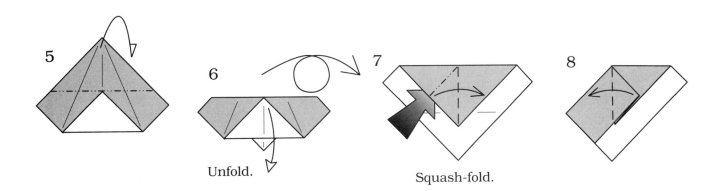

5

6 Unfold.

7 Squash-fold.

8

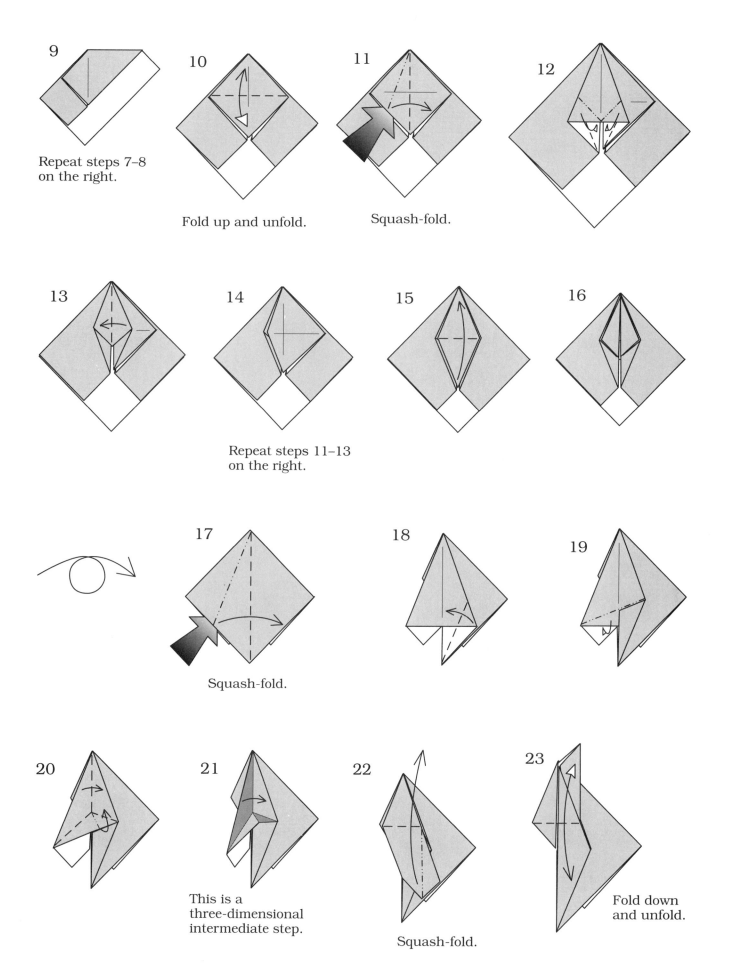

9

Repeat steps 7–8 on the right.

10

Fold up and unfold.

11

Squash-fold.

12

13

14

Repeat steps 11–13 on the right.

15

16

17

Squash-fold.

18

19

20

21

This is a three-dimensional intermediate step.

22

Squash-fold.

23

Fold down and unfold.

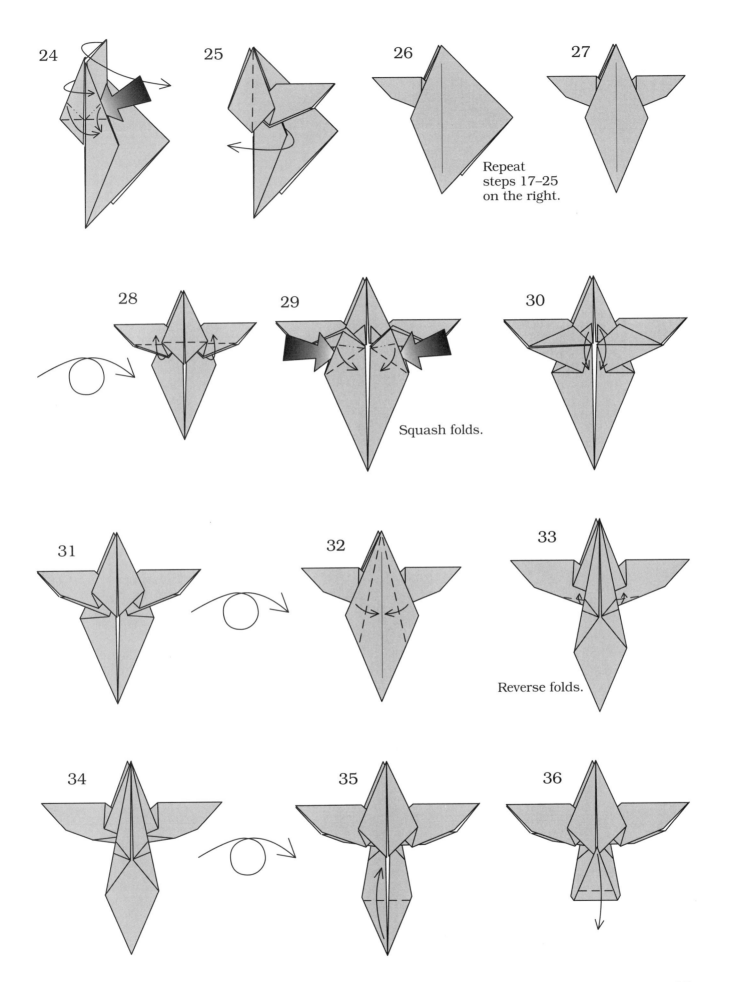

24

25

26

Repeat
steps 17–25
on the right.

27

28

29

Squash folds.

30

31

32

33

Reverse folds.

34

35

36

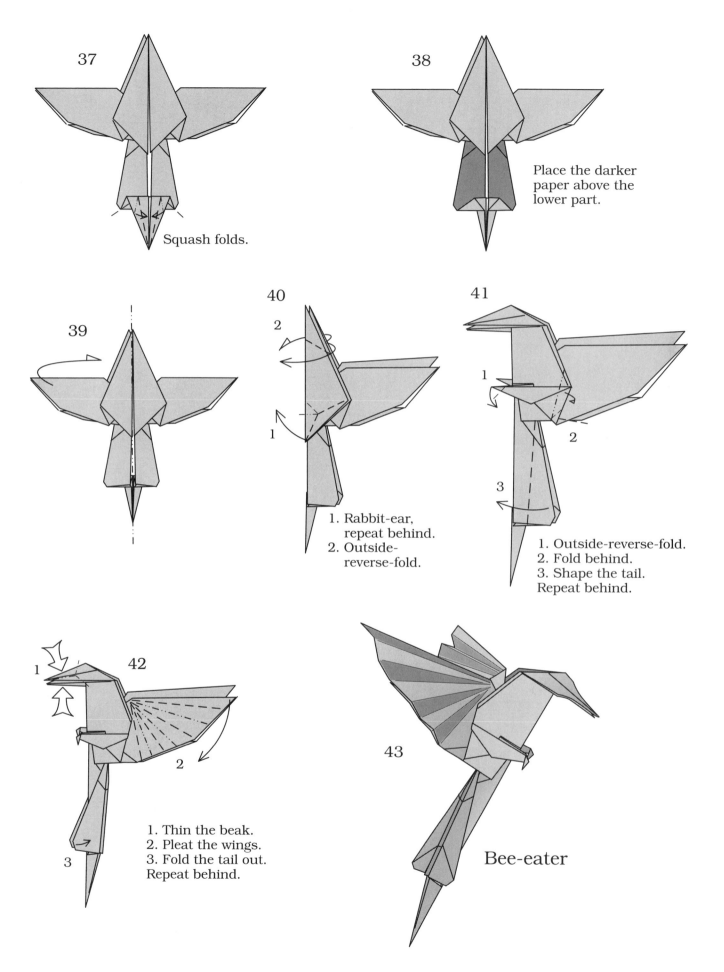

37

Squash folds.

38

Place the darker
paper above the
lower part.

39

40

1. Rabbit-ear,
   repeat behind.
2. Outside-
   reverse-fold.

41

1. Outside-reverse-fold.
2. Fold behind.
3. Shape the tail.
   Repeat behind.

42

1. Thin the beak.
2. Pleat the wings.
3. Fold the tail out.
   Repeat behind.

43

Bee-eater

Hoopoe

The hoopoe, a relative of the hornbill, lives in the warmer portions of Europe, Asia, and Africa. It is most easily distinguished by a handsome crest of feathers which adorns the top of its head and which it raises and lowers when disturbed.

Hoopoes build their nests in trees, wall, and rocks. The female lays 5 to 7 white eggs. While hatching her eggs, the female is fed by the male so she does not have to leave the nest. Hoopoes eat insects, spending much time on the ground searching for them. When frightened, the hoopoe flattens itself to the ground and plays dead.

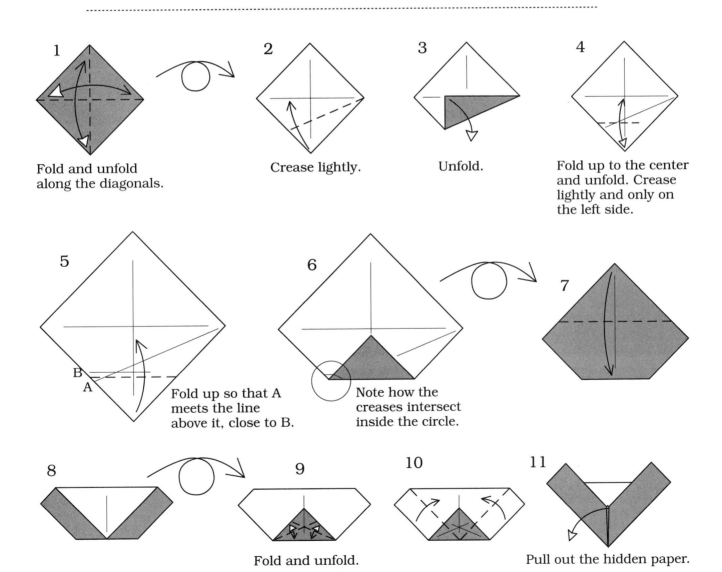

1

Fold and unfold along the diagonals.

2

Crease lightly.

3

Unfold.

4

Fold up to the center and unfold. Crease lightly and only on the left side.

5

B
A

Fold up so that A meets the line above it, close to B.

6

Note how the creases intersect inside the circle.

7

8

9

Fold and unfold.

10

11

Pull out the hidden paper.

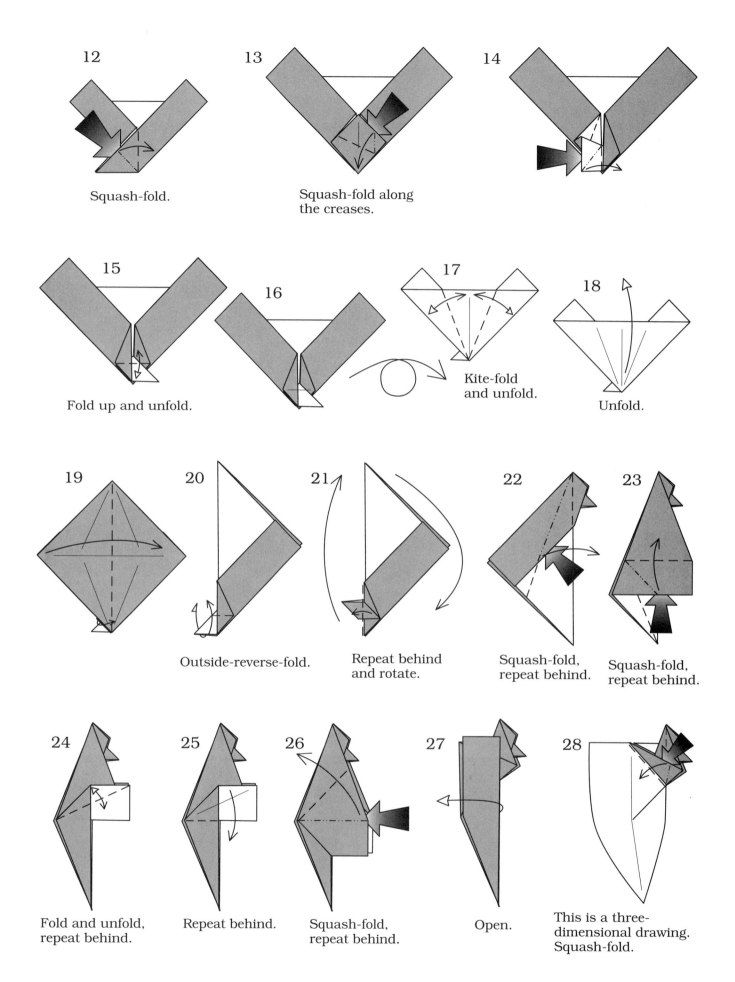

12

Squash-fold.

13

Squash-fold along
the creases.

14

15

Fold up and unfold.

16

17

Kite-fold
and unfold.

18

Unfold.

19

20

Outside-reverse-fold.

21

Repeat behind
and rotate.

22

Squash-fold,
repeat behind.

23

Squash-fold,
repeat behind.

24

Fold and unfold,
repeat behind.

25

Repeat behind.

26

Squash-fold,
repeat behind.

27

Open.

28

This is a three-
dimensional drawing.
Squash-fold.

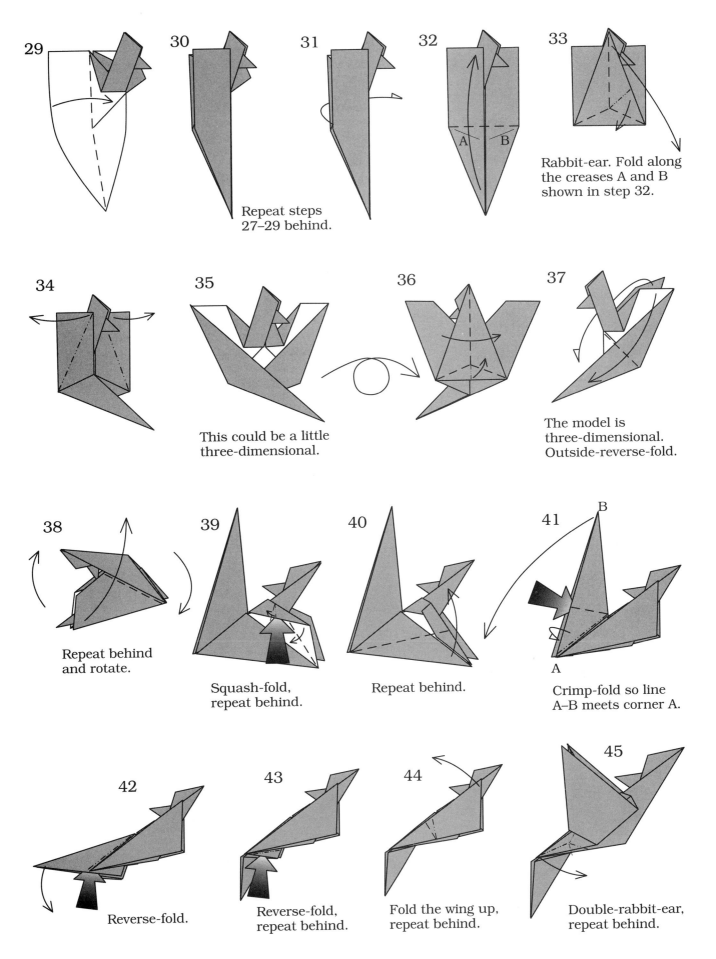

29

30

Repeat steps
27–29 behind.

31

32

A B

33

Rabbit-ear. Fold along
the creases A and B
shown in step 32.

34

35

This could be a little
three-dimensional.

36

37

The model is
three-dimensional.
Outside-reverse-fold.

38

Repeat behind
and rotate.

39

Squash-fold,
repeat behind.

40

Repeat behind.

41

B

A

Crimp-fold so line
A–B meets corner A.

42

Reverse-fold.

43

Reverse-fold,
repeat behind.

44

Fold the wing up,
repeat behind.

45

Double-rabbit-ear,
repeat behind.

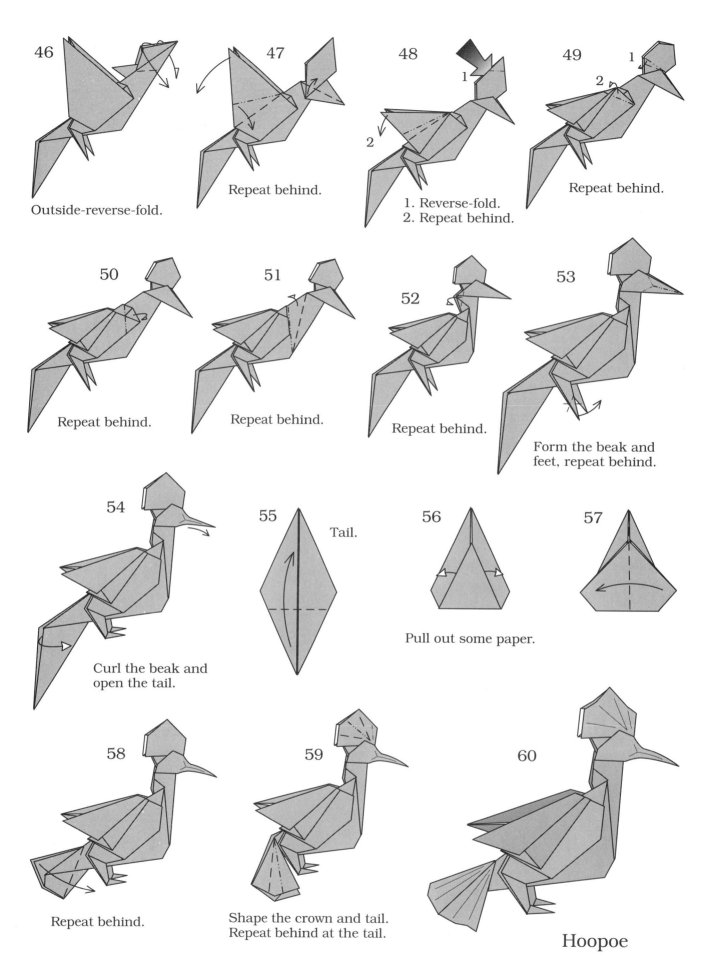

46 Outside-reverse-fold.

47 Repeat behind.

48
1. Reverse-fold.
2. Repeat behind.

49 Repeat behind.

50 Repeat behind.

51 Repeat behind.

52 Repeat behind.

53 Form the beak and feet, repeat behind.

54 Curl the beak and open the tail.

55 Tail.

56 Pull out some paper.

57

58 Repeat behind.

59 Shape the crown and tail. Repeat behind at the tail.

60 Hoopoe

Hornbill

The hornbill is an awkward-looking bird named for its immense, horny bill. It is found in the forests of tropical Africa and Asia. The bill, filled with air cells, has a large base, a pointed end and saw-toothed edges.

Hornbills live in the tops of trees. However, they frequently go to the ground to search for the berries, fruits, and insects that they chiefly feed on. Hornbills also sometimes eat small mammals and reptiles. The females lay their eggs in a hollow tree and remain there until they hatch.

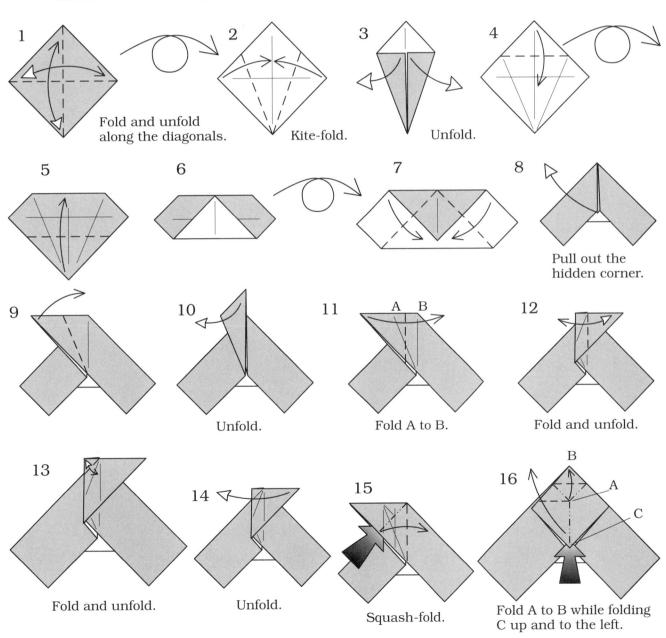

1. Fold and unfold along the diagonals.

2. Kite-fold.

3. Unfold.

4.

5.

6.

7.

8. Pull out the hidden corner.

9.

10. Unfold.

11. A B Fold A to B.

12. Fold and unfold.

13. Fold and unfold.

14. Unfold.

15. Squash-fold.

16. B A C Fold A to B while folding C up and to the left.

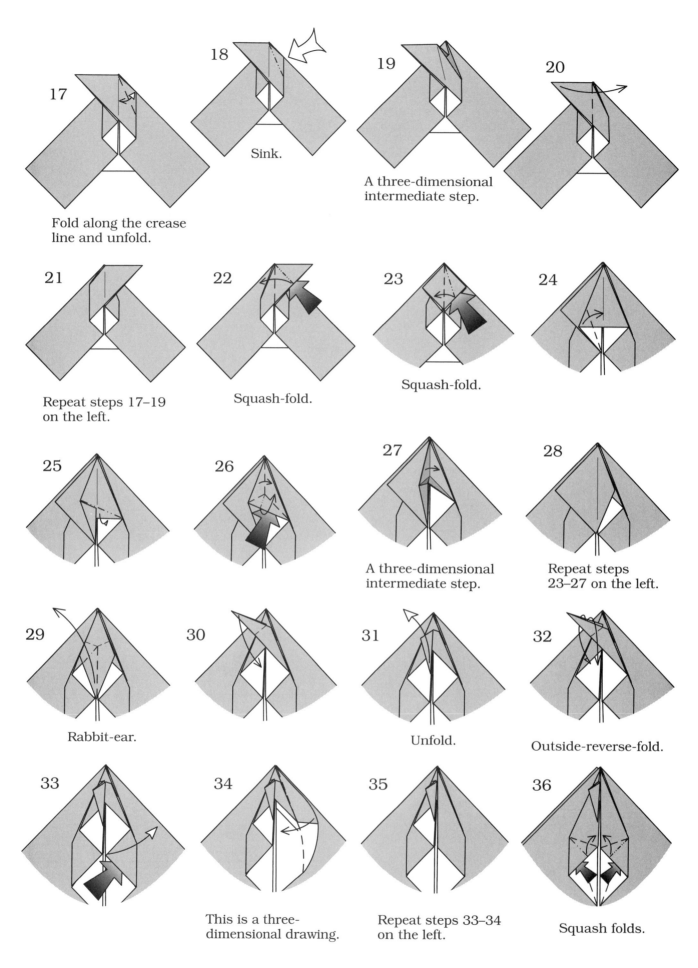

17 Fold along the crease line and unfold.

18 Sink.

19 A three-dimensional intermediate step.

20

21 Repeat steps 17–19 on the left.

22 Squash-fold.

23 Squash-fold.

24

25

26

27 A three-dimensional intermediate step.

28 Repeat steps 23–27 on the left.

29 Rabbit-ear.

30

31 Unfold.

32 Outside-reverse-fold.

33

34 This is a three-dimensional drawing.

35 Repeat steps 33–34 on the left.

36 Squash folds.

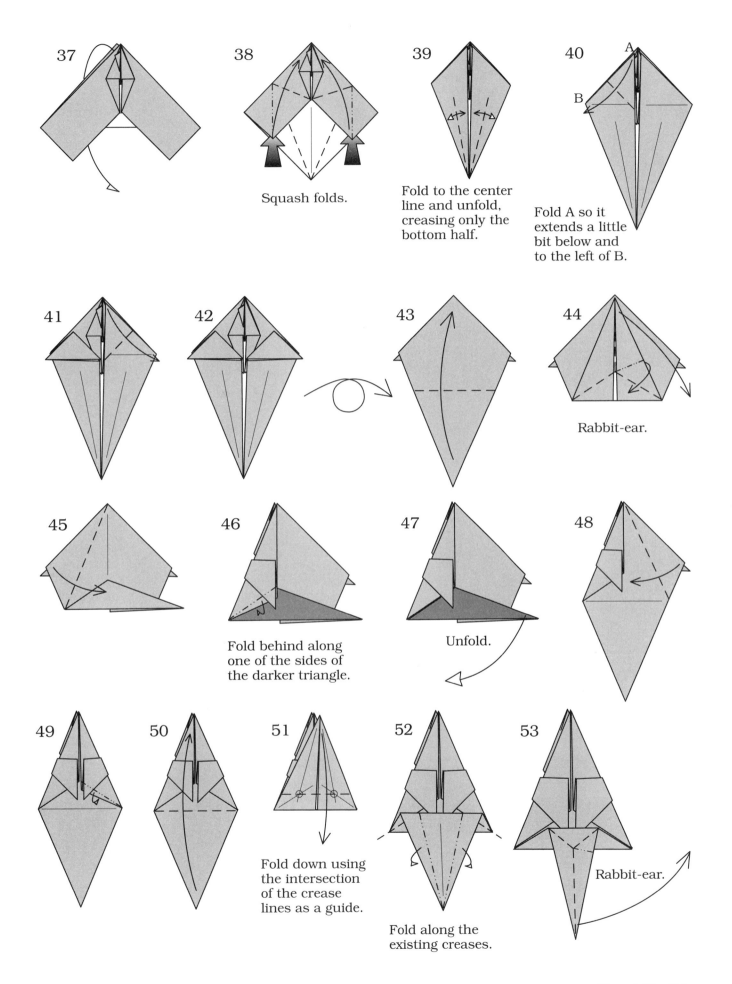

37

38

Squash folds.

39

Fold to the center line and unfold, creasing only the bottom half.

40

A
B

Fold A so it extends a little bit below and to the left of B.

41

42

43

44

Rabbit-ear.

45

46

Fold behind along one of the sides of the darker triangle.

47

Unfold.

48

49

50

51

Fold down using the intersection of the crease lines as a guide.

52

Fold along the existing creases.

53

Rabbit-ear.

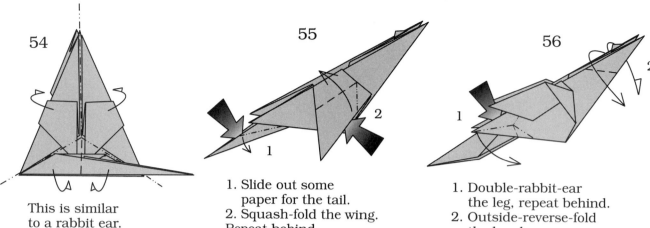

54

This is similar
to a rabbit ear.

55

1. Slide out some
   paper for the tail.
2. Squash-fold the wing.
   Repeat behind.

56

1. Double-rabbit-ear
   the leg, repeat behind.
2. Outside-reverse-fold
   the head.

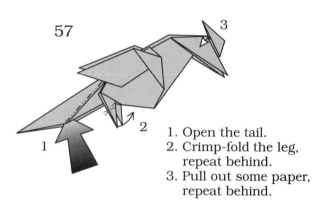

57

1. Open the tail.
2. Crimp-fold the leg,
   repeat behind.
3. Pull out some paper,
   repeat behind.

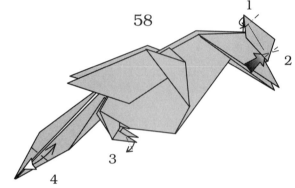

58

1. Reverse-fold.
2. Form the eye with a tiny
   squash-fold, repeat behind.
3. Reverse-fold, repeat behind.
4. Fold the tip of the tail up
   and unfold.

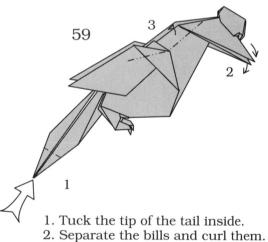

59

1. Tuck the tip of the tail inside.
2. Separate the bills and curl them.
3. Shape the neck and back of body
   to make the hornbill three-
   dimensional, repeat behind.

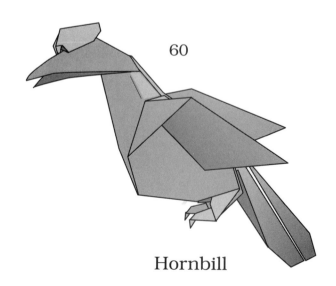

60

Hornbill

Gorilla

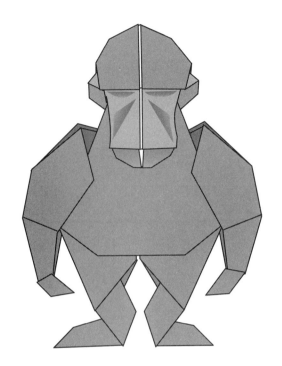

The gorilla is the largest of the apes. Its home is the rain forest of central Africa. The lowland gorilla may be found in western African forests from Nigeria south to the Congo River. Another species, the mountain gorilla, is found in the eastern part of Zaire and western Uganda.

Ranging in weight from 200 to 450 pounds and in height up to 6 feet, the gorilla is a fierce looking animal. It has a shiny black face and large pointed canine teeth. The gorilla's face is characterized by a thick ridge of bone on top of the skull, and a brow ridge above its eyes. The gorilla's foot resemble its hand, for the big toe functions as a "thumb" that aids the gorilla in grasping branches while climbing.

Despite its strength and appearance, the gorilla is actually a gentle animal. It will not attack a human being unless attacked or molested. Like their relatives, the chimpanzees, gorillas are nevertheless friendly animals that need companionship and attention.

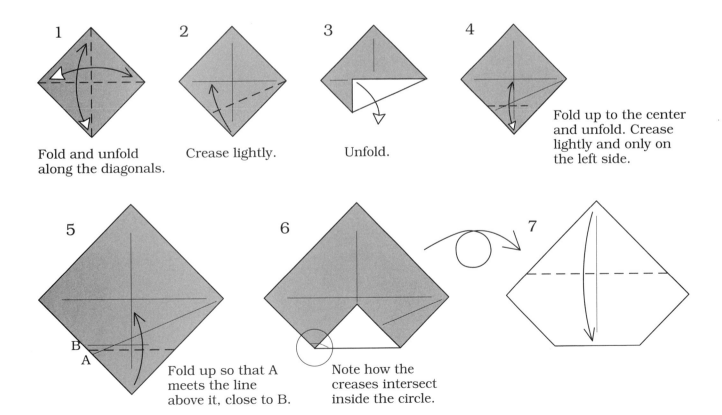

1 Fold and unfold along the diagonals.

2 Crease lightly.

3 Unfold.

4 Fold up to the center and unfold. Crease lightly and only on the left side.

5 Fold up so that A meets the line above it, close to B.

6 Note how the creases intersect inside the circle.

7

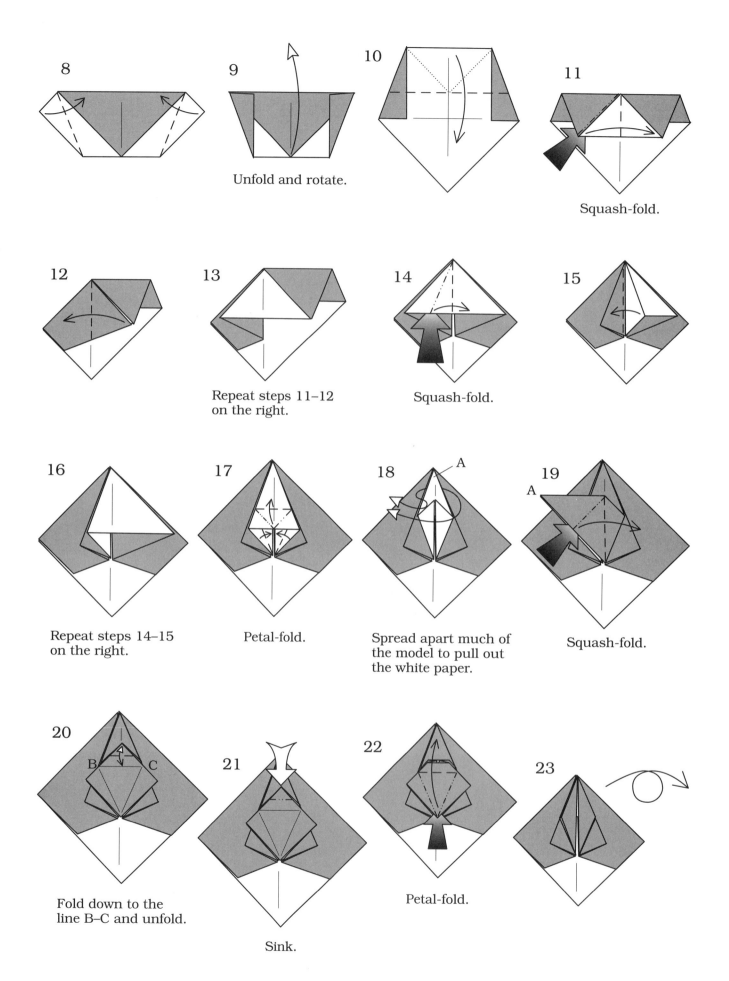

8

9

Unfold and rotate.

10

11

Squash-fold.

12

13

Repeat steps 11–12
on the right.

14

Squash-fold.

15

16

Repeat steps 14–15
on the right.

17

Petal-fold.

18

A

Spread apart much of
the model to pull out
the white paper.

19

A

Squash-fold.

20

B C

Fold down to the
line B–C and unfold.

21

Sink.

22

Petal-fold.

23

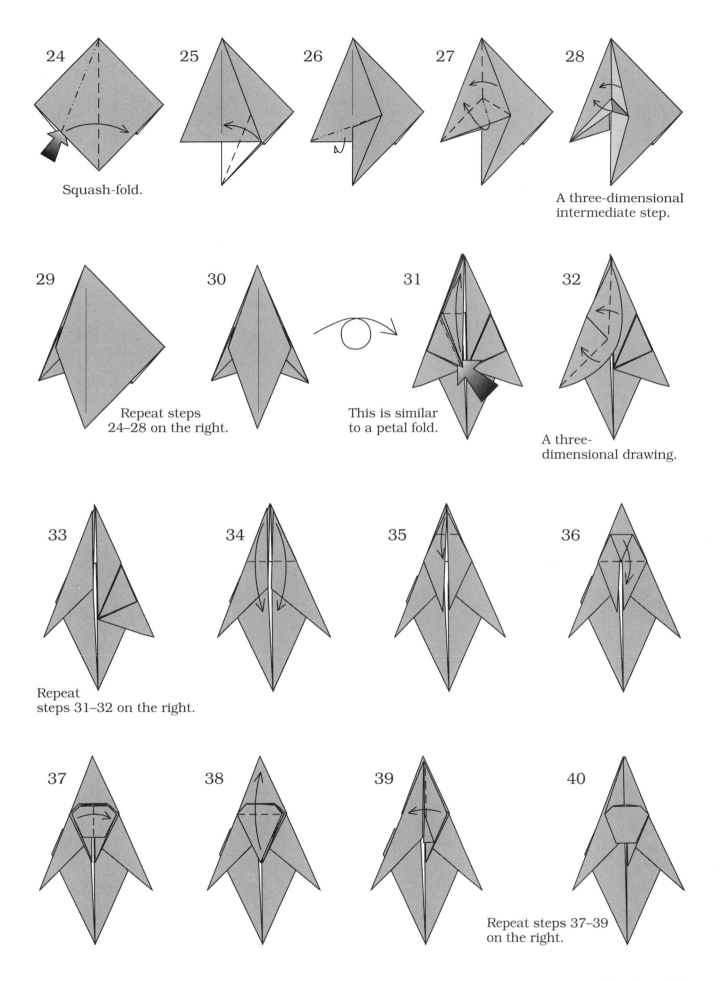

24 Squash-fold.

25

26

27

28 A three-dimensional intermediate step.

29 Repeat steps 24–28 on the right.

30

31 This is similar to a petal fold.

32 A three-dimensional drawing.

33 Repeat steps 31–32 on the right.

34

35

36

37

38

39

40 Repeat steps 37–39 on the right.

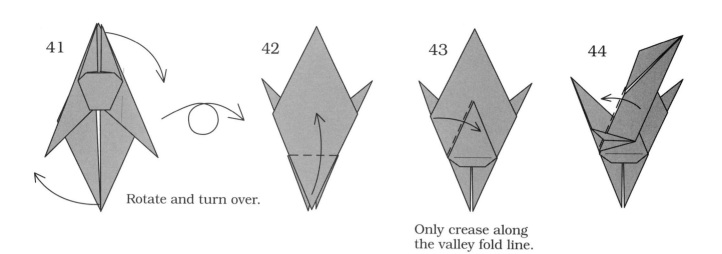

41 Rotate and turn over.

42

43 Only crease along the valley fold line.

44

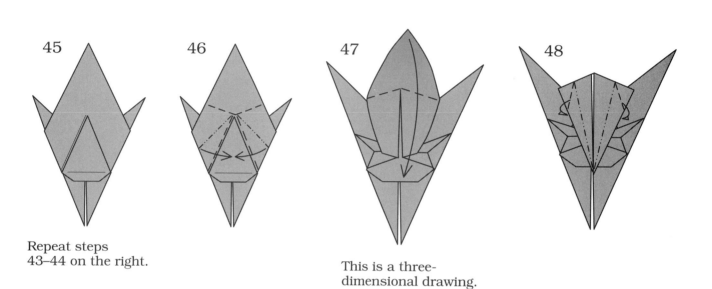

45 Repeat steps 43–44 on the right.

46

47 This is a three-dimensional drawing.

48

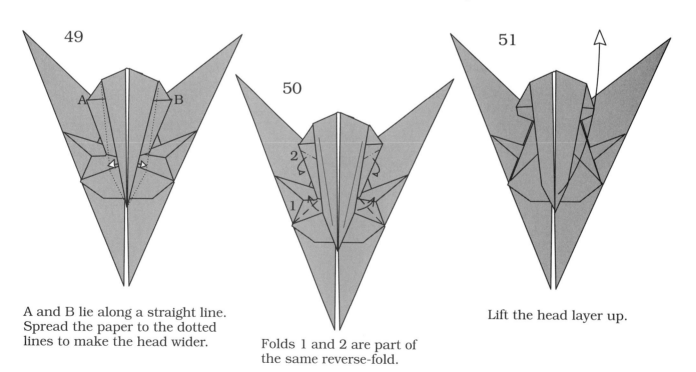

49 A and B lie along a straight line. Spread the paper to the dotted lines to make the head wider.

50 Folds 1 and 2 are part of the same reverse-fold.

51 Lift the head layer up.

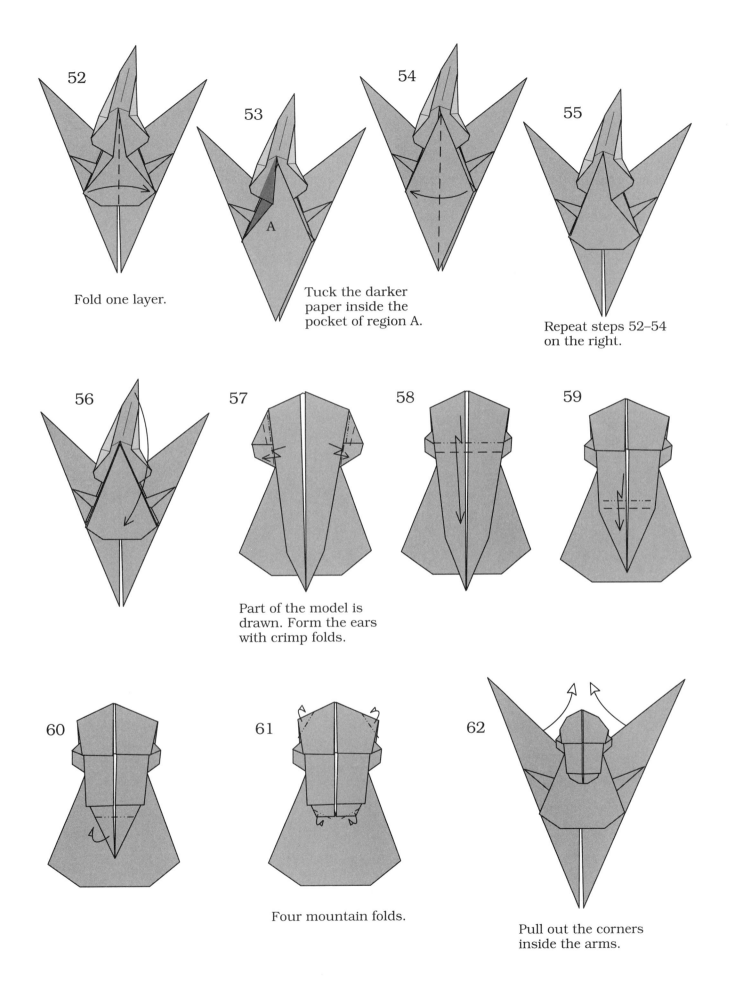

52

Fold one layer.

53

Tuck the darker
paper inside the
pocket of region A.

54

55

Repeat steps 52–54
on the right.

56

57

Part of the model is
drawn. Form the ears
with crimp folds.

58

59

60

61

Four mountain folds.

62

Pull out the corners
inside the arms.

Gorilla 57

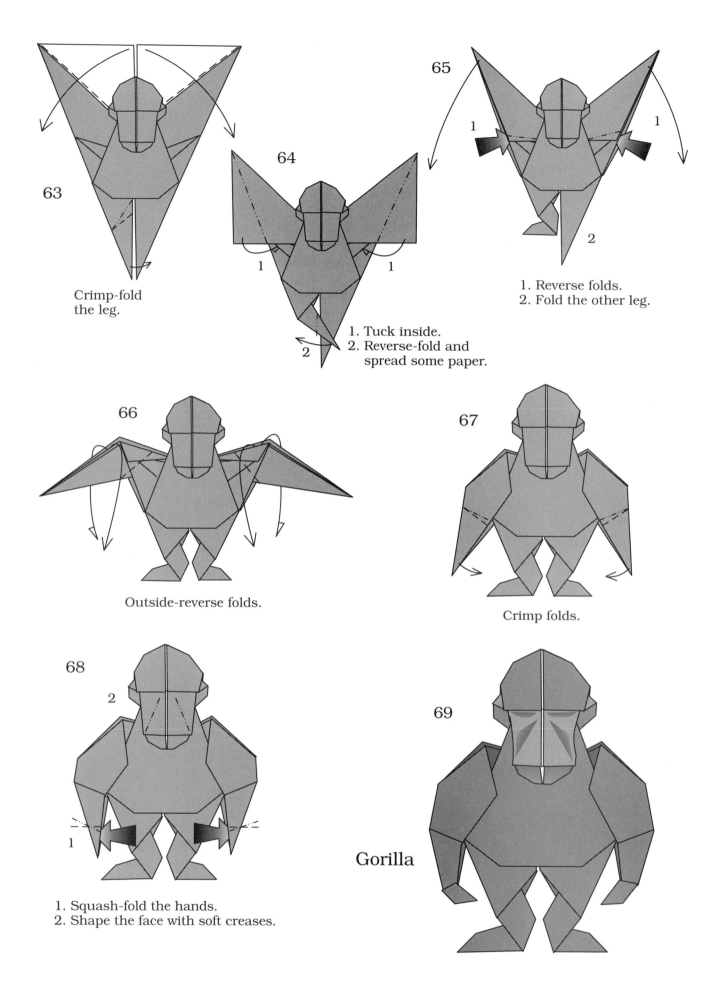

63

Crimp-fold
the leg.

64

1. Tuck inside.
2. Reverse-fold and
   spread some paper.

65

1. Reverse folds.
2. Fold the other leg.

66

Outside-reverse folds.

67

Crimp folds.

68

1. Squash-fold the hands.
2. Shape the face with soft creases.

69

Gorilla

Chimpanzee

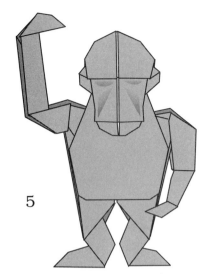

5

The chimpanzee is a member of the ape family. The common chimpanzee inhabits much of Central Africa, from Lake Victoria in the east to Sierra Leone in the west. The rarer, pygmy chimpanzee lives only in Zaire, south of the Congo River and west of the Luabala River.

The chimpanzee has many characteristics that are interesting, valuable and endearing to humans. Chimpanzees are naturally playful and curious. They are easily tamed and trained.

Chimpanzees range in height from over 3 feet to 5 and a half feet and in weight from 90 to 110 pounds. The chimpanzee's body is covered with long black hair and, like other apes, has no tail. The chimpanzee has large ears and its arms are longer than its legs. The chimpanzee's hands suit it well for grasping and holding objects. On their feet, the big toes face sideways like thumbs allowing chimpanzees to grasp objects and branches while climbing.

Begin with step 66 of the Gorilla on page 53.

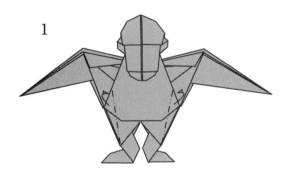

1

Repeat behind.

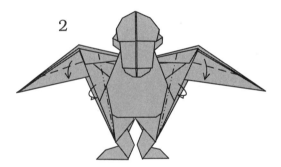

2

Repeat behind.

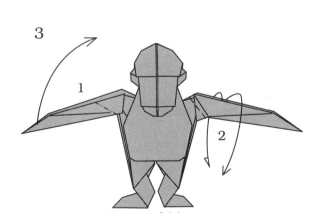

3

1. Reverse-fold.
2. Outside-reverse-fold.

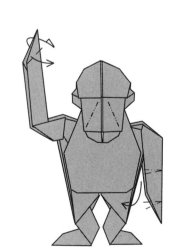

4

Shape the arms, hands, and head.

African Elephant

African elephants are the largest living land mammals. They are harder to train than their smaller (and smaller-eared) Indian cousins and so are seldom used for labor or seen in circuses.

Elephants have prehensile trunks, ivory tusks that incite poachers to kill over 100,000 of the great beasts annually, and floppy ears which are crisscrossed with blood vessels. Elephants wave their ears to cool the blood in them, which in turn circulates to cool the rest of the body.

The massive beasts require a tremendous amount of vegetation daily. Their appetites sculpt African ecosystems. Elephants will knock over trees to get to the tender top parts, and a hungry herd will turn a forest into open grassland.

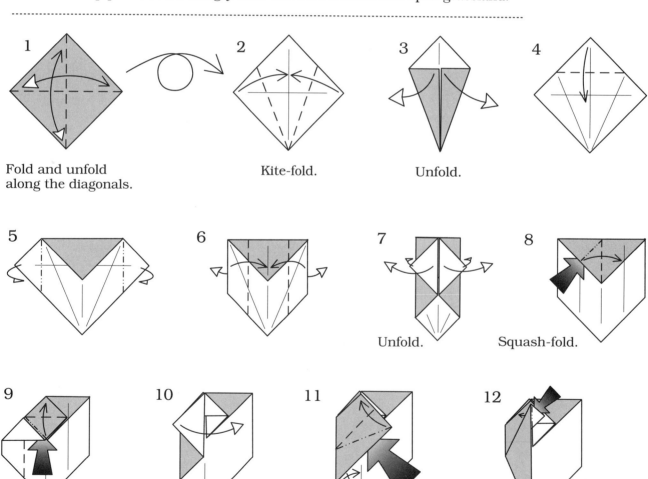

1 Fold and unfold along the diagonals.

2 Kite-fold.

3 Unfold.

4

5

6

7 Unfold.

8 Squash-fold.

9 Squash-fold.

10 Unfold.

11 Squash-fold.

12 Reverse-fold.

13

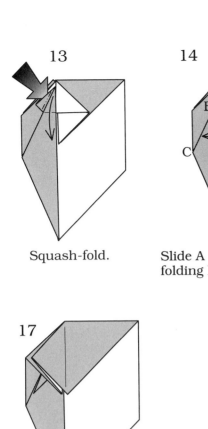

Squash-fold.

14

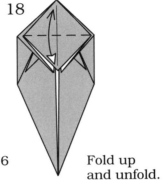

Slide A to line B–C while folding D down.

15

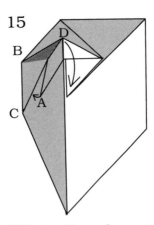

This is a three-dimensional intermediate step.

16

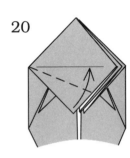

17

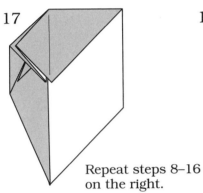

Repeat steps 8–16 on the right.

18

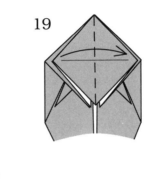

Fold up and unfold.

19

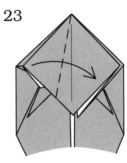

20

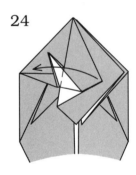

21

22

This is a three-dimensional step.

23

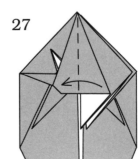

Squash-fold the tusk.

24

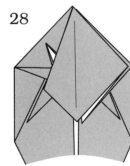

25

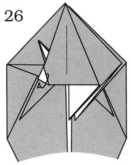

Squash-fold.

26

Fold the white corner inside-out.

27

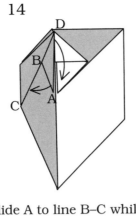

28

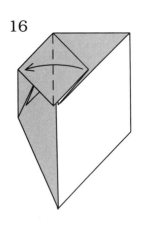

Repeat steps 19–27 on the right.

African Elephant 61

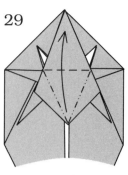

29

Petal-fold.

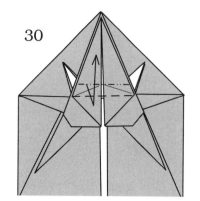

30

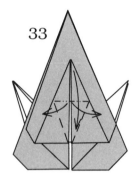

31

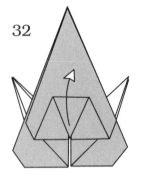

32

Unfold.

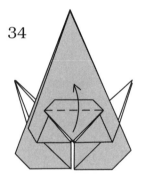

33

Open.

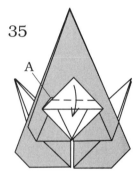

34

35

A

The valley line is sightly below line A.

36

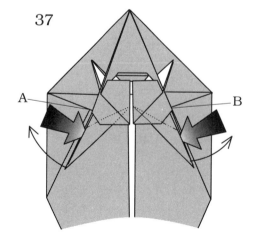

37

A ——————— B

The edges will meet A and B for these reverse folds.

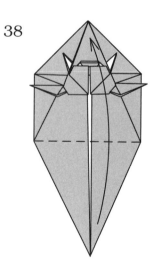

38

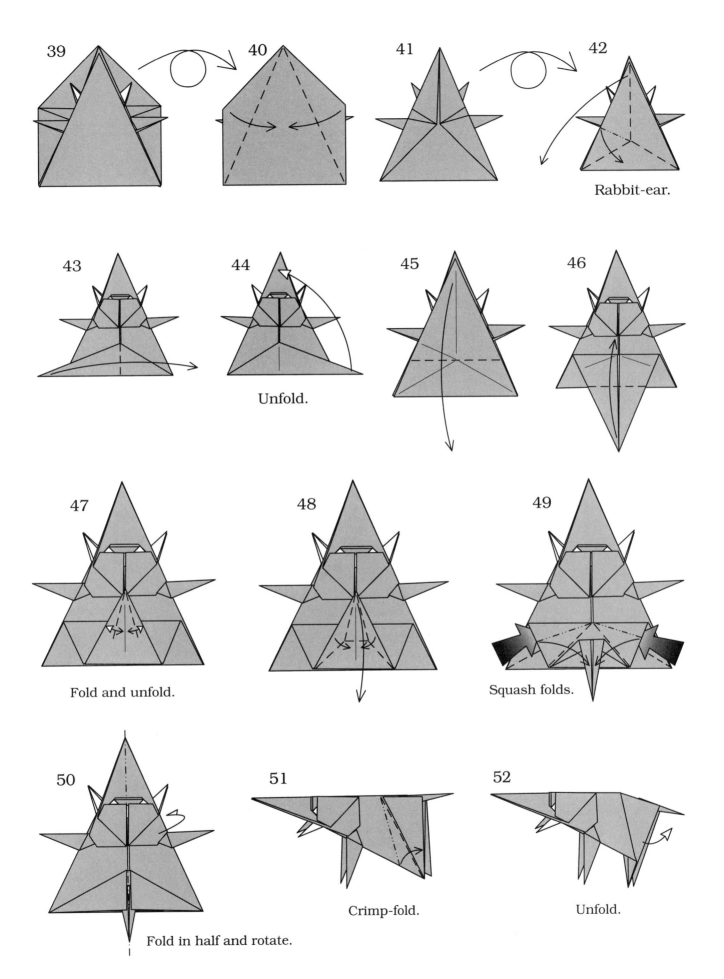

39

40

41

42

Rabbit-ear.

43

44

Unfold.

45

46

47

Fold and unfold.

48

49

Squash folds.

50

Fold in half and rotate.

51

Crimp-fold.

52

Unfold.

African Elephant 63

53

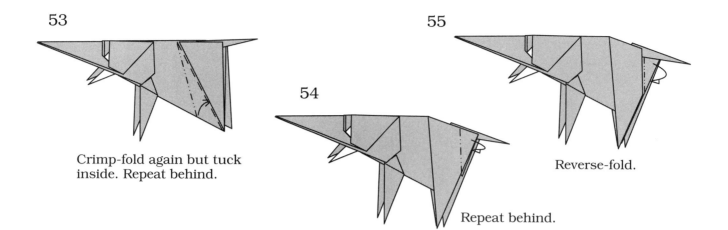

Crimp-fold again but tuck
inside. Repeat behind.

54

Repeat behind.

55

Reverse-fold.

56

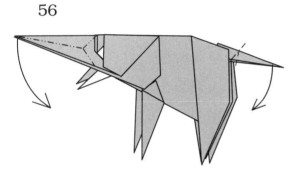

Crimp-fold the tail.
Double-rabbit-ear the trunk.

57

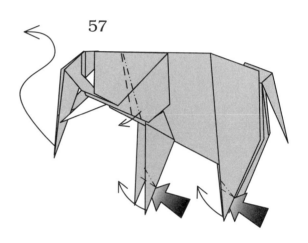

Shape the trunk with reverse folds.
Pleat-fold the ears. Crimp-fold the
feet. Repeat behind.

58

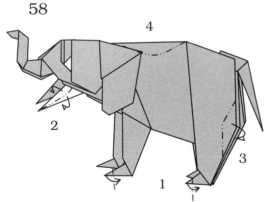

4

2

3

1

1. Reverse-fold the feet.
2. Thin and curl the tusks.
3. Make the hind legs three-
   dimensional.
4. Make the body three-
   dimensional.
Repeat behind.

59

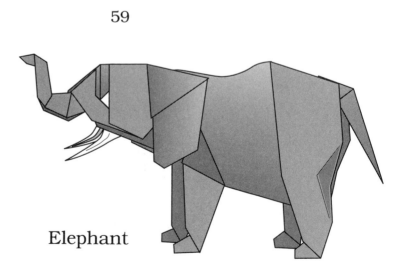

Elephant

In the Savanna

The rolling grassland called the African savanna extends 3,000 miles from the Atlantic to the Indian Ocean.

The average annual rainfall varies from 20 to 60 inches over the vast savanna. Because temperatures rarely dip below 70° F and because the rain is concentrated during one part of the year, even the best-watered sections of the savanna are often parched and dusty. The annual drought ends when climactic downpours begin the wet season. The savanna's rebirth takes only a few days. Savanna grasses, adapted to the cyclic climate, may grow an inch a day when the rains start. The savanna's occasional trees and coarse shrubs soak up the water and bloom.

The sudden abundance of vegetation draws a huge variety of life. Great herds of zebras, gnus, antelopes, and other grazers crowd the plains. Giraffes and elephants share the uppermost buds of the trees. Lions, cheetahs, leopards, and other carnivores await their opportunity. Circling vultures are the final link in the food cycle.

When the rains end and the savanna dries up once again, the animals begin their long marches to wetter and greener regions. The grasses die and trees drop their leaves. Then come the dry-season fires, kindled by lightning. Eventually the storm clouds will gather to wash the ash-borne nutrients back into the soil and to bring back the green splendor of the savanna.

Ostrich

The ostrich is the world's largest living bird. It may stand nearly 8 feet tall and weigh as much as 345 pounds. Ostriches populate the plains and deserts of Africa. The ostrich was exceeded in height only by the now extinct moas of New Zealand, which were 10 feet tall. Only the now-extinct elephant birds of Madagascar, weighing about 1,000 pounds, were heavier than the ostrich.

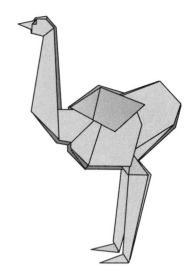

The ostrich is a handsome bird. It has black feathers covering its bulky body with large, white feathers or plumes on its small wings and tail. However, there are virtually no feathers on its long, thin legs, upper neck, and small head. The bare skin may vary in color from pink to blue. Thick black eyelashes surround its eyes. Female ostriches have dull brown feathers. The ostrich is also unique in that it is the only bird with two toes on each foot.

The wings of the ostrich are too small to carry it in flight. Therefore, the ostrich relies on its long legs for locomotion. The ostrich is known for its running speed which may reach up to 40 miles per hour. The ostrich makes good use of this speed and its unusually good eyesight to keep away from its enemies which include lions and humans. There is no truth to the myth that an ostrich buries its head in the sand when frightened. If exhausted or cornered into defending its nest, the ostrich will kick with its powerful legs. The ostrich's long toes (the longer of which may reach 7 inches long) end in thick nails that the ostrich may effectively use as dangerous weapons.

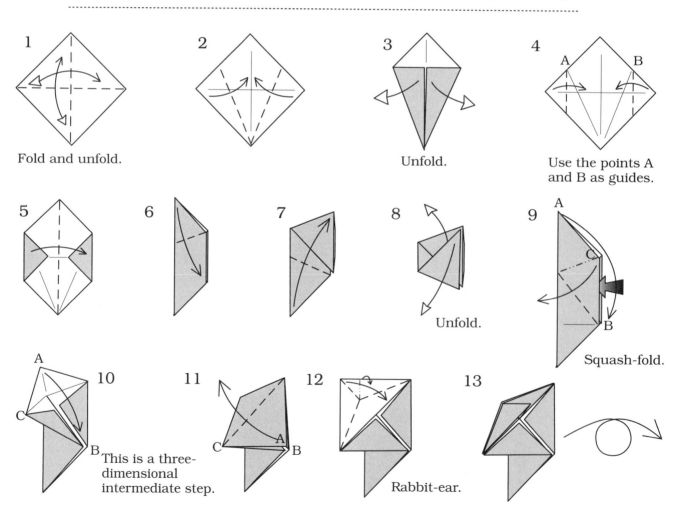

1. Fold and unfold.

2.

3. Unfold.

4. Use the points A and B as guides.

5.

6.

7.

8. Unfold.

9. Squash-fold.

10. This is a three-dimensional intermediate step.

11.

12. Rabbit-ear.

13.

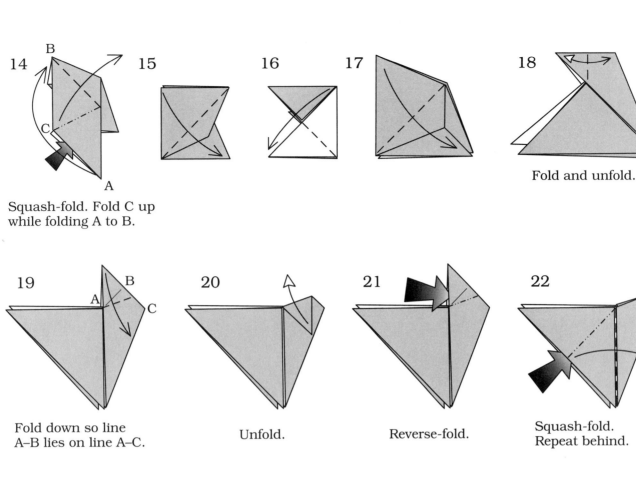

14 Squash-fold. Fold C up while folding A to B.

15

16

17

18 Fold and unfold.

19 Fold down so line A–B lies on line A–C.

20 Unfold.

21 Reverse-fold.

22 Squash-fold. Repeat behind.

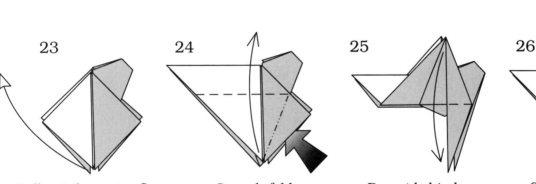

23 Pull out the center flap.

24 Squash-fold. Repeat behind.

25 Repeat behind.

26 Spread the paper while folding up.

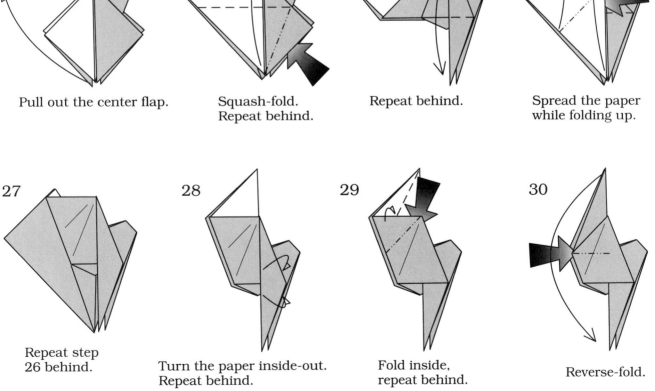

27 Repeat step 26 behind.

28 Turn the paper inside-out. Repeat behind.

29 Fold inside, repeat behind.

30 Reverse-fold.

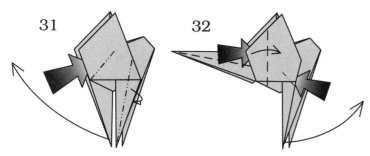

31

Reverse-fold the
neck. Repeat
behind at the leg.

32

Squash-fold the neck.
Reverse-fold the leg.
Repeat behind.

33

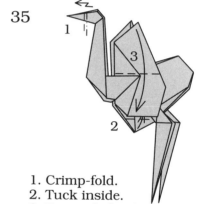

Outside-reverse-fold the neck.
Thin the leg, repeat behind.

34

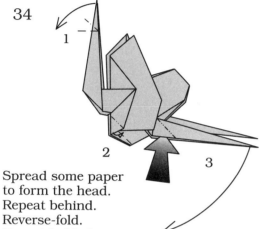

1. Spread some paper
   to form the head.
2. Repeat behind.
3. Reverse-fold.
   Repeat behind.

35

1. Crimp-fold.
2. Tuck inside.
3. Repeat behind.

36

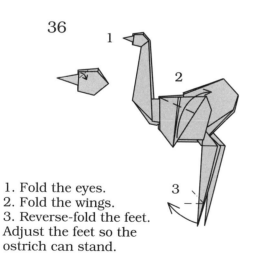

1. Fold the eyes.
2. Fold the wings.
3. Reverse-fold the feet.
   Adjust the feet so the
   ostrich can stand.

37

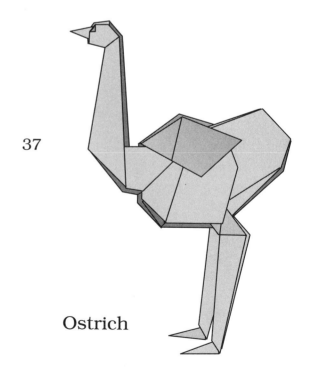

Ostrich

Vulture

Vulture is the name given to several large birds of prey that feed on carrion. Alone among birds of prey, vultures have no feathers on their head. They also have slightly hooked bills and blunt claws which serve as poor weapons for carrying off their food. Vultures are found in temperate to tropical regions of America, Europe, Africa, and Asia. New World vultures belong to their own distinct family of birds, Old World vultures are members of the hawk family.

Although a macabre and menacing sight at close range, vultures are graceful in flight, soaring high on updrafts to hunt for dead animals. Their heads, naked of feathers, do not easily pick up particles from their culinary finds, and vultures do not carry disease. In fact, they prevent its spread by clearing away carcasses that would otherwise decay and cause health problems.

1
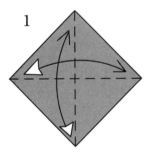

Fold and unfold along the diagonals.

2
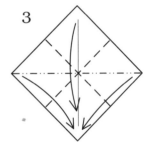

Fold and unfold.

3
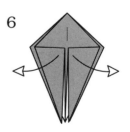

Collapse the square by bringing the four corners together.

4

This is a three-dimensional intermediate step.

5

Kite-fold, repeat behind.

6
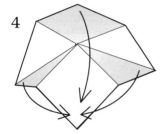

Unfold, repeat behind.

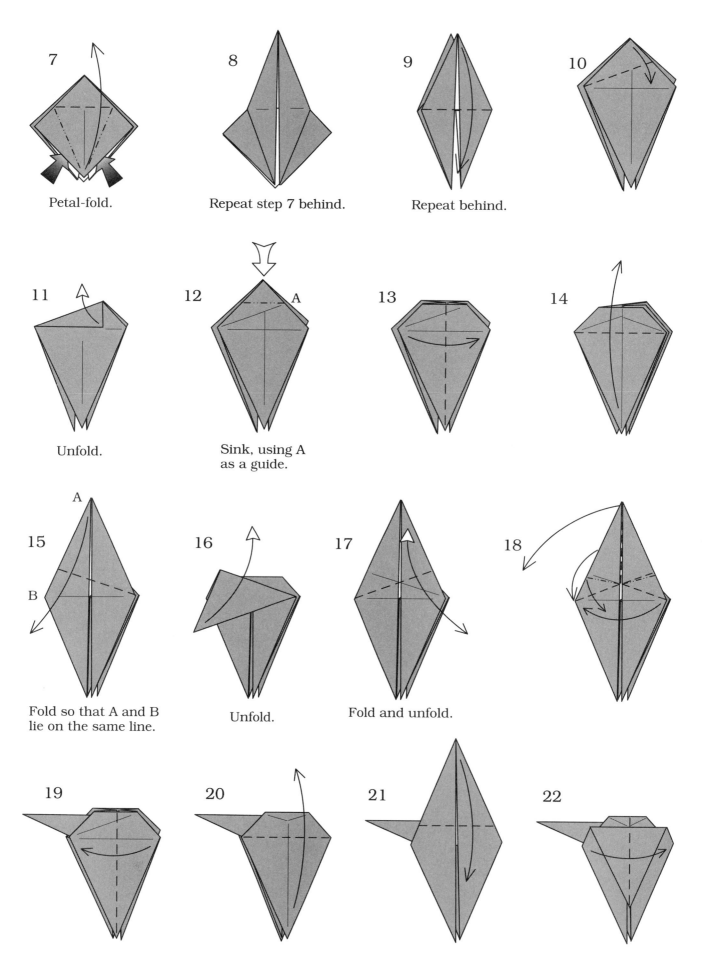

7
Petal-fold.

8
Repeat step 7 behind.

9
Repeat behind.

10

11
Unfold.

12
Sink, using A as a guide.

13

14

15
Fold so that A and B lie on the same line.

16
Unfold.

17
Fold and unfold.

18

19

20

21

22

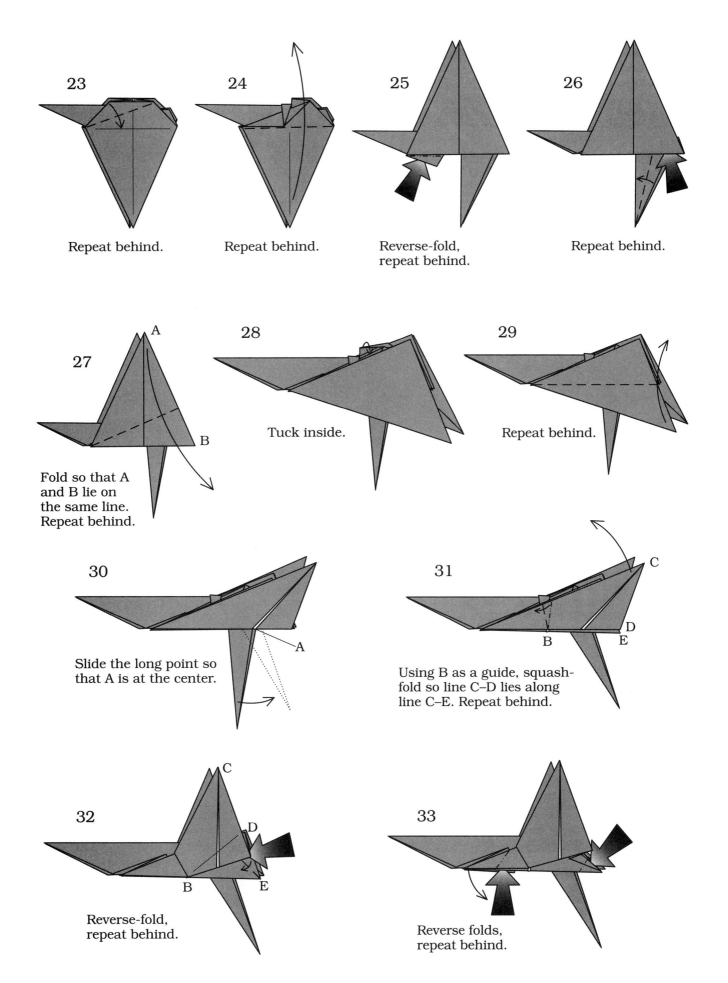

23

Repeat behind.

24

Repeat behind.

25

Reverse-fold,
repeat behind.

26

Repeat behind.

27

A

B

Fold so that A
and B lie on
the same line.
Repeat behind.

28

Tuck inside.

29

Repeat behind.

30

A

Slide the long point so
that A is at the center.

31

C

B

D

E

Using B as a guide, squash-
fold so line C–D lies along
line C–E. Repeat behind.

32

C

D

B

E

Reverse-fold,
repeat behind.

33

Reverse folds,
repeat behind.

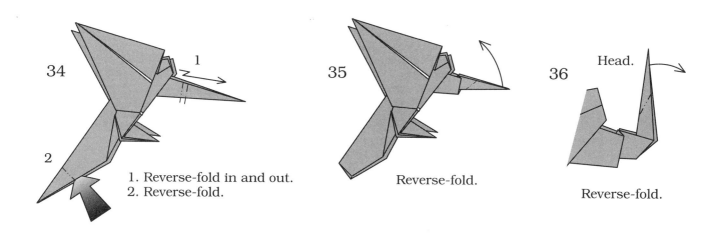

34

1. Reverse-fold in and out.
2. Reverse-fold.

35

Reverse-fold.

36 Head.

Reverse-fold.

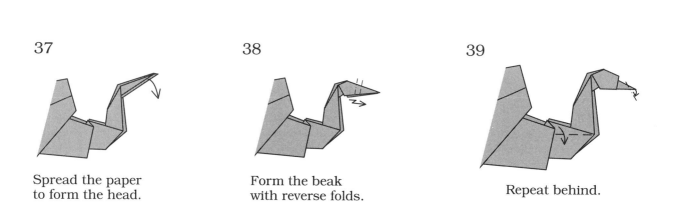

37

Spread the paper to form the head.

38

Form the beak with reverse folds.

39

Repeat behind.

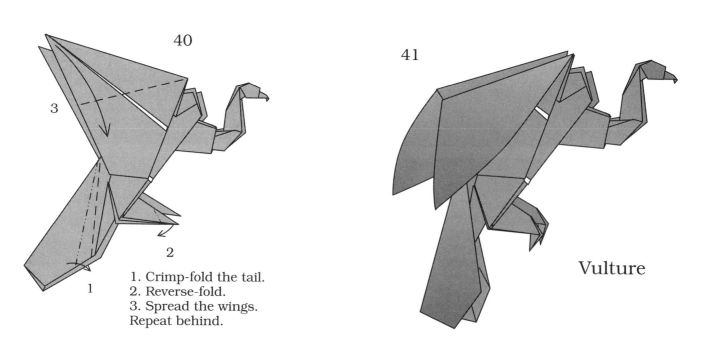

40

3

1

2

1. Crimp-fold the tail.
2. Reverse-fold.
3. Spread the wings.
Repeat behind.

41

Vulture

Aardvark

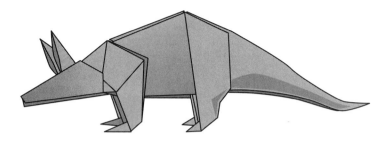

The aardvark is an African mammal that lives in the ground and feeds on insects and termites. The animal's name, which means "earth pig," was given to the animal in the early 1600's by Dutch settlers in Africa.

The aardvark measures six to eight feet from the tip of its snout to the end of its tail and weighs about 140 pounds. Its skin is covered by a thin coat of hair. Its short front legs are armed with four short claws while the longer hind legs have five claws. These claws enable the aardvark to tear open the nests of ants and termites upon which it feeds. Then, it catches the insects with its long sticky tongue which may reach up to 18 inches in length.

The aardvark also uses its claws to dig its home. Few animals can dig as fast as the aardvark, which can dig a deep hole and escape from its enemies in a matter of minutes. The aardvark usually hunts alone at night, spending most of the day sleeping.

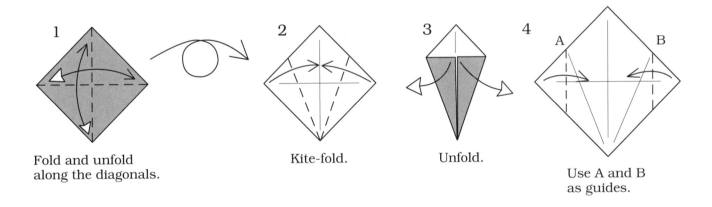

1
Fold and unfold along the diagonals.

2
Kite-fold.

3
Unfold.

4
A   B
Use A and B as guides.

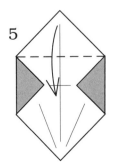

5

6

7
Unfold.

8

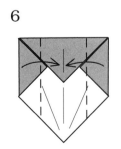

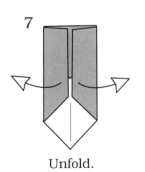

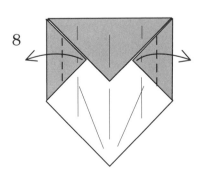

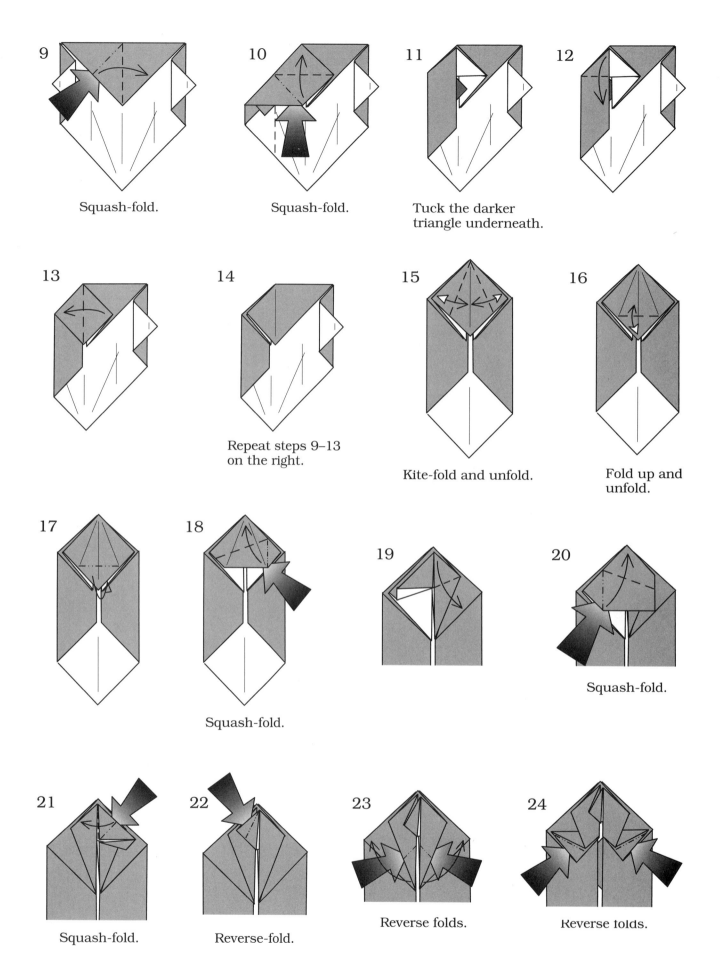

9 Squash-fold.

10 Squash-fold.

11 Tuck the darker triangle underneath.

12

13

14 Repeat steps 9–13 on the right.

15 Kite-fold and unfold.

16 Fold up and unfold.

17

18 Squash-fold.

19

20 Squash-fold.

21 Squash-fold.

22 Reverse-fold.

23 Reverse folds.

24 Reverse folds.

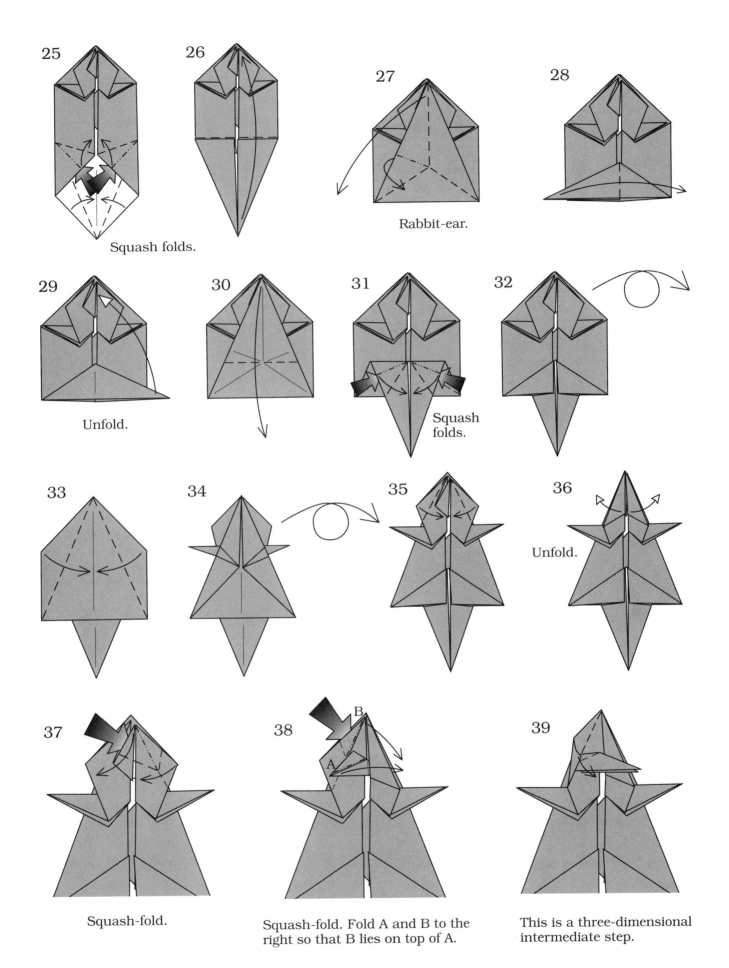

25

26

27
Rabbit-ear.

28

29
Unfold.

30

31
Squash folds.

32

33

34

35

36
Unfold.

37
Squash-fold.

38
Squash-fold. Fold A and B to the right so that B lies on top of A.

39
This is a three-dimensional intermediate step.

Squash folds.

Aardvark 75

40

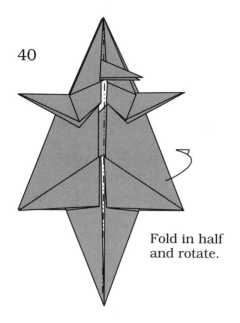

Fold in half and rotate.

41

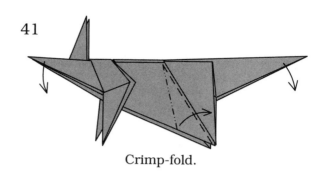

Crimp-fold.

42

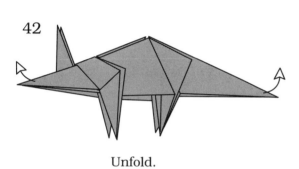

Unfold.

43

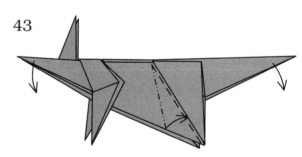

Crimp-fold again but tuck inside. Repeat behind.

44

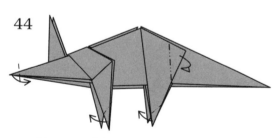

Reverse-fold the tip of the nose and the feet. Repeat behind.

45

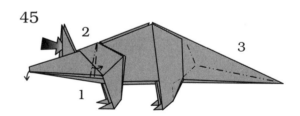

1. Crimp the neck.
2. Open the ears.
3. Shape the tail and hind legs with soft creases.

46

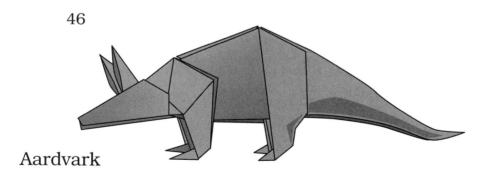

Aardvark

Rhinoceros

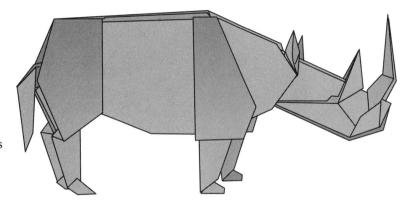

The rhinoceros is one of the largest land animals. Its immense, solid, and almost hairless body is covered by loose rough skin. The legs are short and clumsy but powerful. The animal's name, which means "nose-horned" in Greek, is derived from the one or two (depending on species) slightly curved horns that grow from the long snout.

The wild rhino lives on a diet of grass, leafy twigs, and shrubs. In captivity, rhinos eat hay and a dietary supplement of proteins, vitamins, and minerals. Wild rhinos may be found in Africa, southern Asia, and a few large islands near the Asiatic coast. The ancestors of the rhinoceros may also have roamed over Europe, North America, and northern Asia.

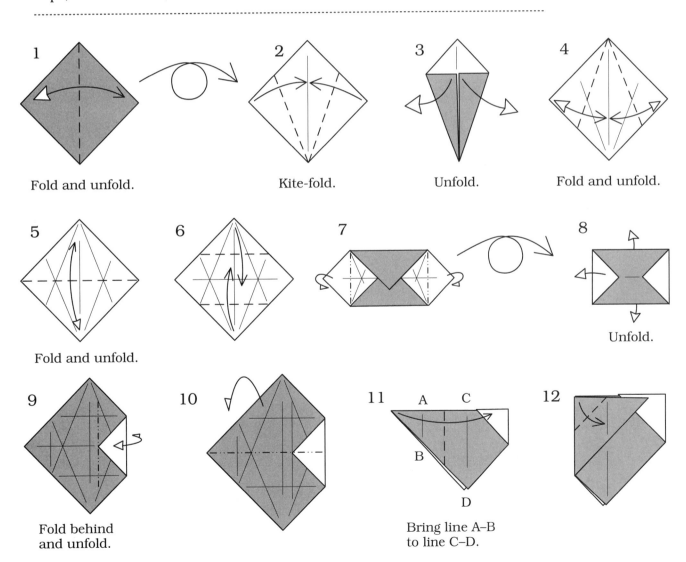

1 Fold and unfold.

2 Kite-fold.

3 Unfold.

4 Fold and unfold.

5 Fold and unfold.

6

7

8 Unfold.

9 Fold behind and unfold.

10

11 Bring line A–B to line C–D.

12

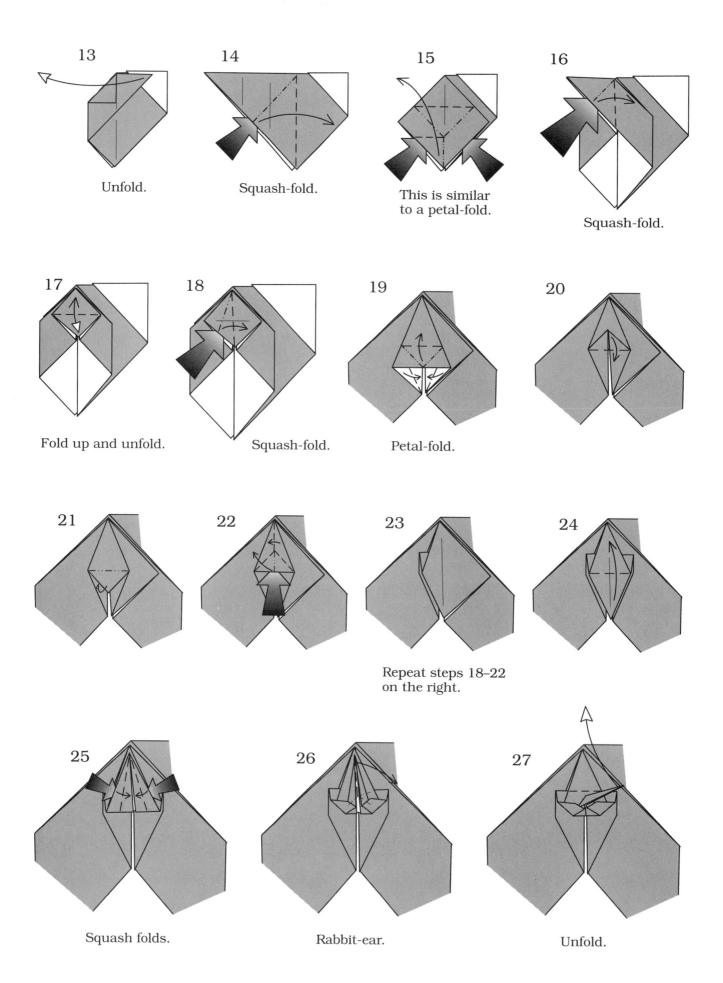

13 Unfold.

14 Squash-fold.

15 This is similar to a petal-fold.

16 Squash-fold.

17 Fold up and unfold.

18 Squash-fold.

19 Petal-fold.

20

21

22

23 Repeat steps 18–22 on the right.

24

25 Squash folds.

26 Rabbit-ear.

27 Unfold.

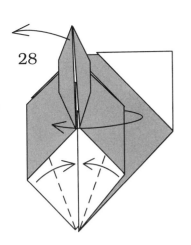

28

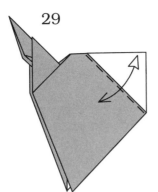

29

Fold and unfold.

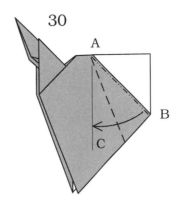

30

Fold line A–B
to line A–C,
repeat behind.

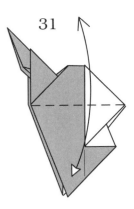

31

Fold up and unfold,
repeat behind.

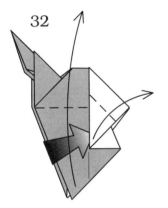

32

Squash-fold,
repeat behind.

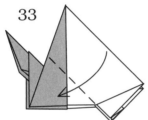

33

Repeat behind.

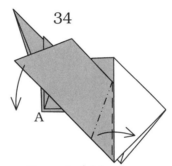

34

Squash-fold
so the edge meets
corner A. Repeat
behind.

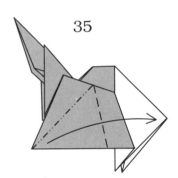

35

Squash-fold,
repeat behind.

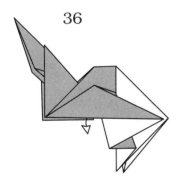

36

Pull out paper from
inside, repeat behind.

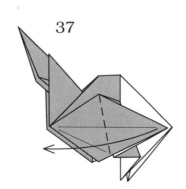

37

Repeat behind.

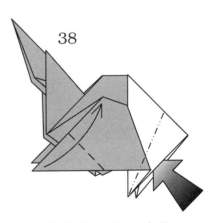

38

Squash-fold at the tail. Repeat
behind at the front leg.

Rhinoceros 79

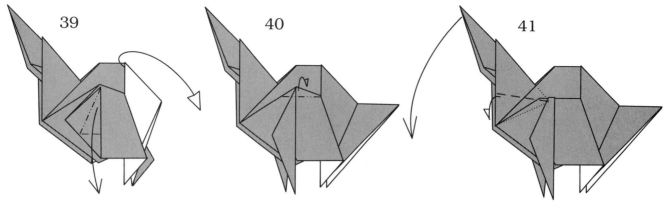

39

Pull out the tail. Squash-fold the front leg, repeat behind.

40

Fold along the crease, repeat behind.

41

Slide the neck down, this is similar to a crimp fold.

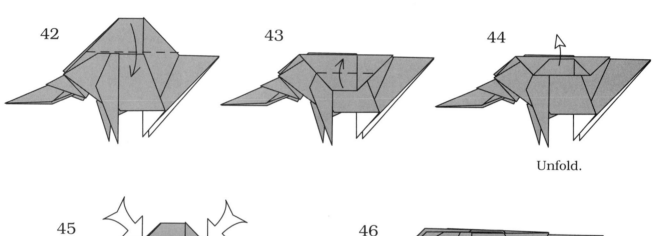

42

43

44

Unfold.

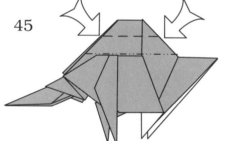

45

Sink down and up.

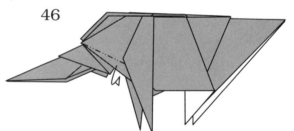

46

Fold behind along the crease, repeat behind.

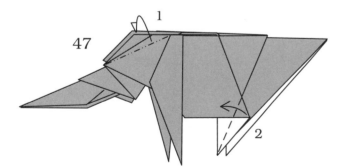

47

Fold both layers behind together at (1). Repeat behind.

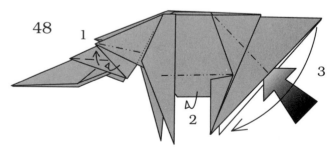

48

1. Reverse-fold, repeat behind.
2. Repeat behind.
3. Reverse-fold.

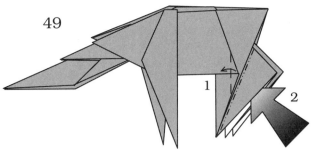

49

Reverse-fold by the
tail. Repeat behind.

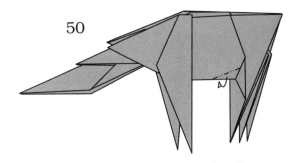

50

Repeat behind.

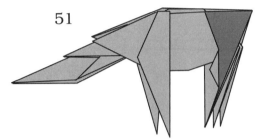

51

Place the darker region on top.

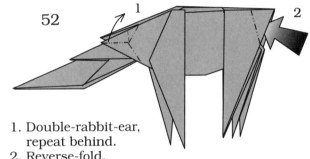

52

1. Double-rabbit-ear,
   repeat behind.
2. Reverse-fold.

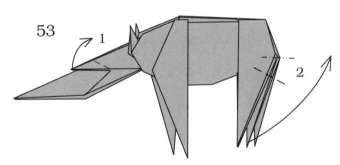

53

1. Outside-reverse-fold the horn.
2. Fold the tail up.

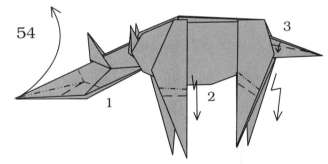

54

1. Form the large horn by
   refolding steps 24–26.
2. Shape the legs with reverse
   folds, repeat behind.
3. Thin the tail, repeat behind.

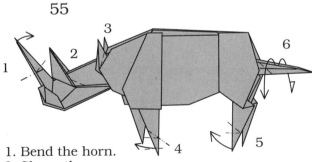

55

1. Bend the horn.
2. Shape the eye.
3. Open the ear.
4. Reverse-folds.
5. Spread to form the
   hooves on the hind legs.
6. Outside-reverse-fold.
Repeat behind.

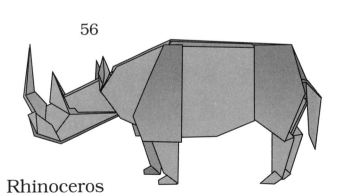

56

Rhinoceros

Gazelle

The gazelle is a slender antelope known for its beauty, gentleness, and grace. The name gazelle comes from an Arabic word which means "to be affectionate". There are about 25 species of gazelle which may be found over a vast area of northern and eastern Africa and Asia. In these regions, gazelles may inhabit mountain ranges but often prefers open, sandy plains.

Gazelles are plant-eating animals. They are especially known as fast runners. Some have been able to outrun even the swiftest greyhounds. Hunters thus set traps, snares, or enclosures near watering places to trap gazelles when they stop to drink. Such hunting has resulted in the classification of 10 species of gazelles as endangered. Gazelle populations are also endangered by cattle herds which eat most of the vegetation in the open plains where gazelles graze.

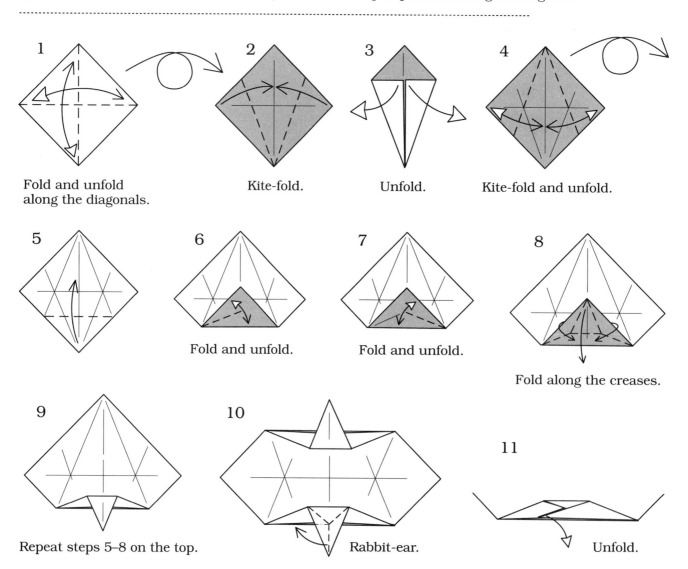

1 Fold and unfold along the diagonals.

2 Kite-fold.

3 Unfold.

4 Kite-fold and unfold.

5

6 Fold and unfold.

7 Fold and unfold.

8 Fold along the creases.

9 Repeat steps 5–8 on the top.

10 Rabbit-ear.

11 Unfold.

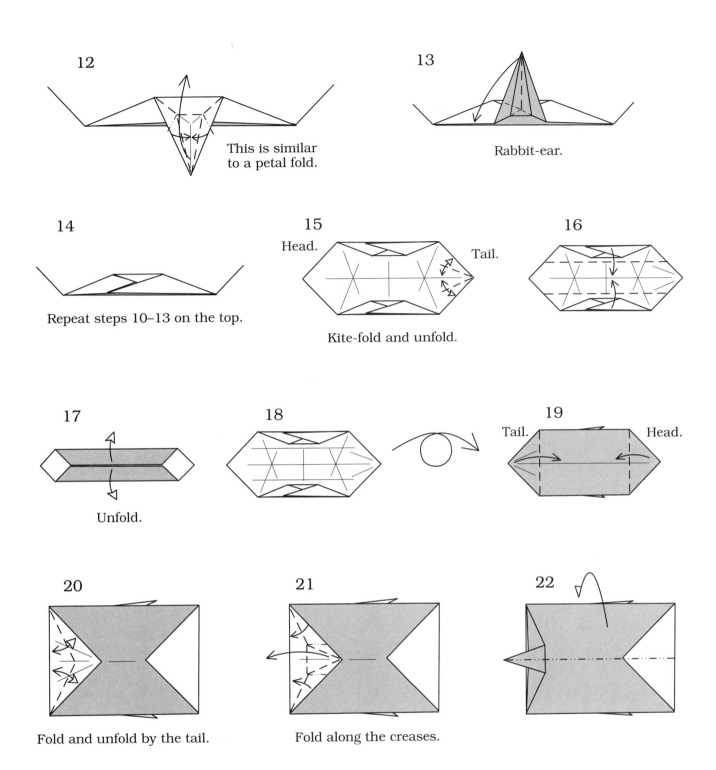

12

This is similar to a petal fold.

13

Rabbit-ear.

14

Repeat steps 10–13 on the top.

15

Head.

Tail.

Kite-fold and unfold.

16

17

Unfold.

18

19

Tail.

Head.

20

Fold and unfold by the tail.

21

Fold along the creases.

22

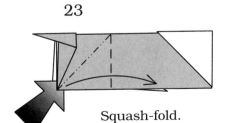

23

Squash-fold.

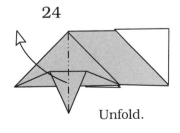

24

Unfold.

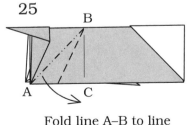

25

B

A   C

Fold line A–B to line B–C, repeat behind.

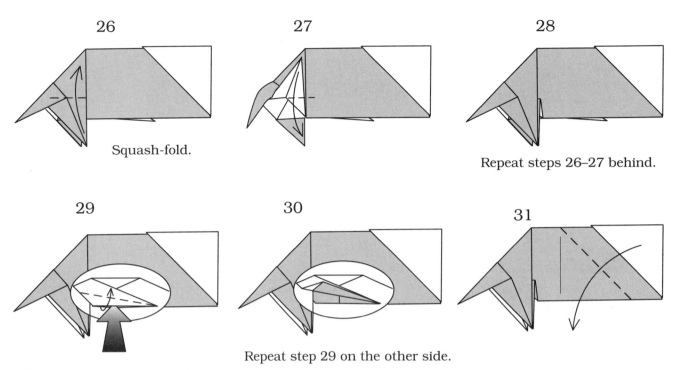

26

27

Squash-fold.

28

Repeat steps 26–27 behind.

29

The oval uncovers an inside view.
Unlock some paper for this fold.

30

Repeat step 29 on the other side.

31

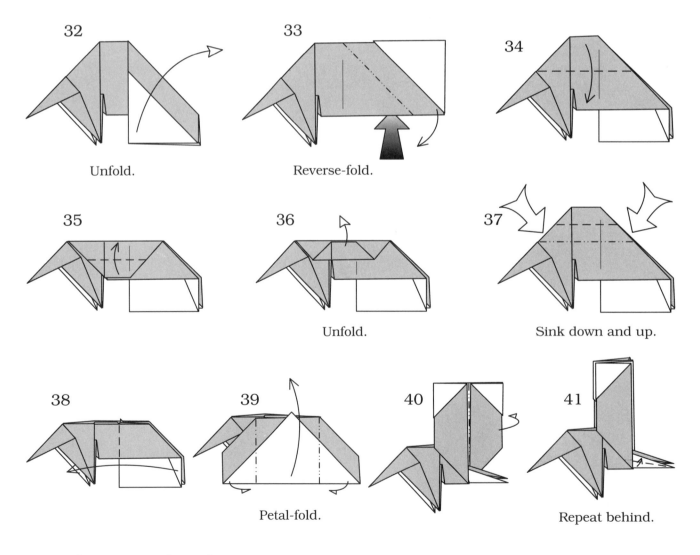

32

Unfold.

33

Reverse-fold.

34

35

36

Unfold.

37

Sink down and up.

38

39

Petal-fold.

40

41

Repeat behind.

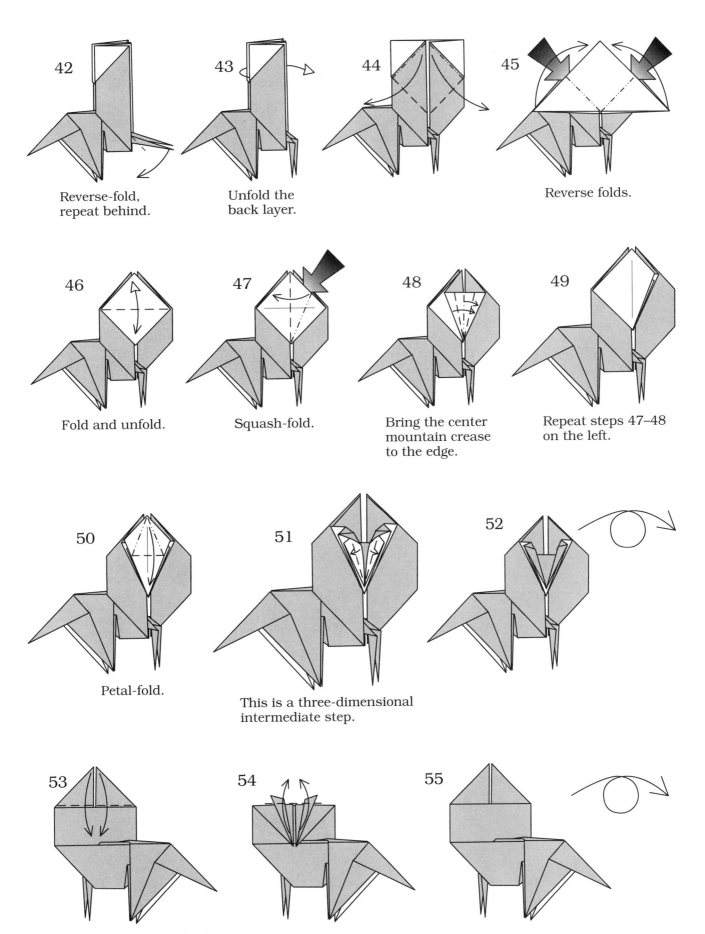

42 Reverse-fold, repeat behind.

43 Unfold the back layer.

44

45 Reverse folds.

46 Fold and unfold.

47 Squash-fold.

48 Bring the center mountain crease to the edge.

49 Repeat steps 47–48 on the left.

50 Petal-fold.

51 This is a three-dimensional intermediate step.

52

53 This is similar to steps 50–51.

54

55

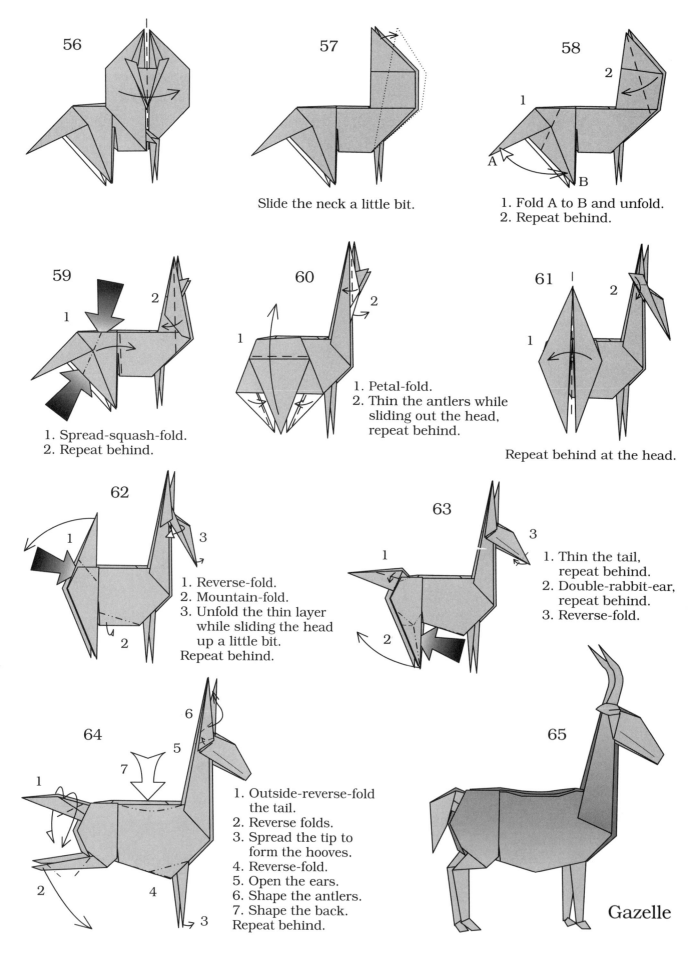

56

57

Slide the neck a little bit.

58

A

B

1. Fold A to B and unfold.
2. Repeat behind.

59

1
2

1. Spread-squash-fold.
2. Repeat behind.

60

1
2

1. Petal-fold.
2. Thin the antlers while
   sliding out the head,
   repeat behind.

61

1
2

Repeat behind at the head.

62

1
2
3

1. Reverse-fold.
2. Mountain-fold.
3. Unfold the thin layer
   while sliding the head
   up a little bit.
Repeat behind.

63

1
2
3

1. Thin the tail,
   repeat behind.
2. Double-rabbit-ear,
   repeat behind.
3. Reverse-fold.

64

1
2
4
5
6
7
3

1. Outside-reverse-fold
   the tail.
2. Reverse folds.
3. Spread the tip to
   form the hooves.
4. Reverse-fold.
5. Open the ears.
6. Shape the antlers.
7. Shape the back.
Repeat behind.

65

Gazelle

Lion

The lion is a very large and powerful cat. It is perhaps the most well-known member of the cat family. The strength, fierceness, and royal appearance of these animals has struck both fear and respect in the hearts of both men and other beasts. The lion is thus commonly referred to as the "king of beasts" as a symbol of its beauty and power.

Lions may be found both in cool climates and semidesert areas. They shun forests, instead preferring woodlands, grassy plains and areas with thorny scrub trees. Lions live where they may find a supply of food—chiefly deer, antelope, zebra, and other hoofed animals—and a source of water. In ancient times lions were to be found in Europe, the Middle East, India, and much of Africa. However, because of the spread of man, hunting has all but eliminated the lion population in the Middle East and northern Africa. There are only about 200 lions in Asia, all in India. Lions may still be found wild in east and central Africa. However, most are found either in national parks and reserves or in captivity in zoos worldwide.

Unlike other big cats, the lion is built for strength, not speed. It weighs from 350–500 pounds and grows to be almost nine feet long from nose to tail and three and a half feet tall at the shoulder. It is the only cat with a mane. The mane not only makes the lion look bigger than it actually is but it also protects the lion by absorbing the blows of its foes. Lions are also distinguished by their brownish yellow coat, ideal for hiding in dead grass. They have tremendously muscular shoulders and forelegs which allow them to grasp and hold down their prey. Each heavy paw is armed with curved retractable claws that make the lion a most formidable hunter.

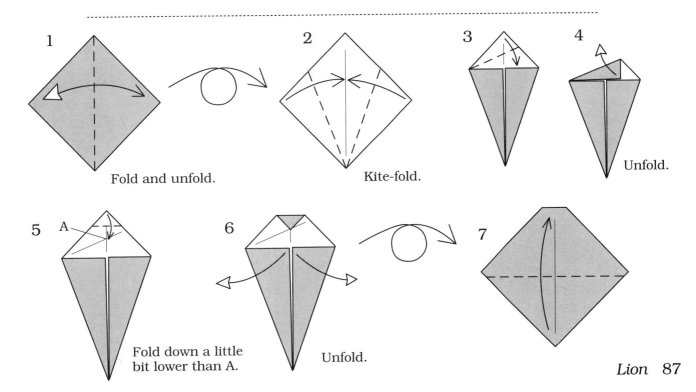

1 Fold and unfold.

2 Kite-fold.

3

4 Unfold.

5 A Fold down a little bit lower than A.

6 Unfold.

7

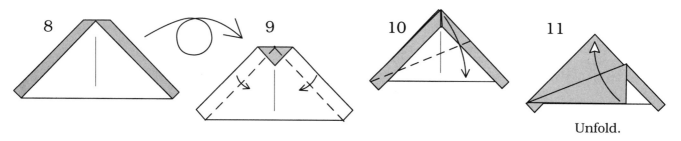

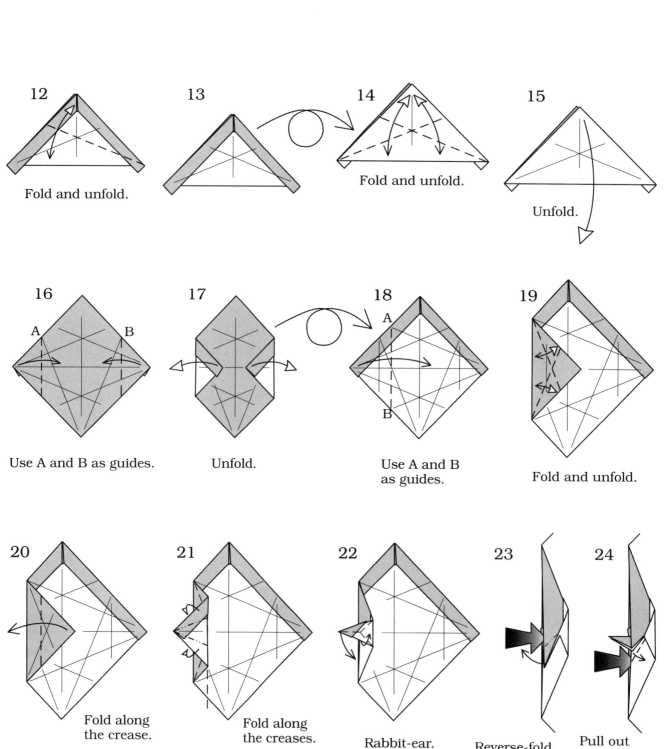

8

9

10

11

Unfold.

12

Fold and unfold.

13

14

Fold and unfold.

15

Unfold.

16

A   B

Use A and B as guides.

17

Unfold.

18

A

B

Use A and B
as guides.

19

Fold and unfold.

20

Fold along
the crease.

21

Fold along
the creases.

22

Rabbit-ear.

23

Reverse-fold.

24

Pull out
some paper.

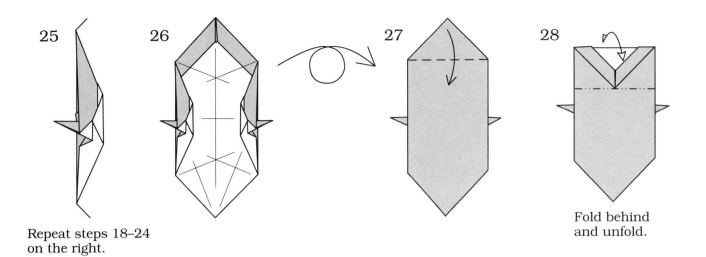

25

Repeat steps 18–24 on the right.

26

27

28

Fold behind and unfold.

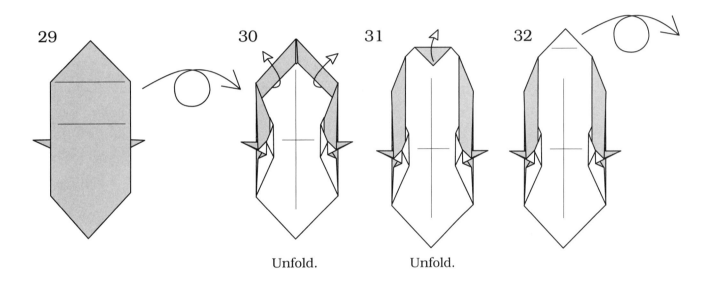

29

30

Unfold.

31

Unfold.

32

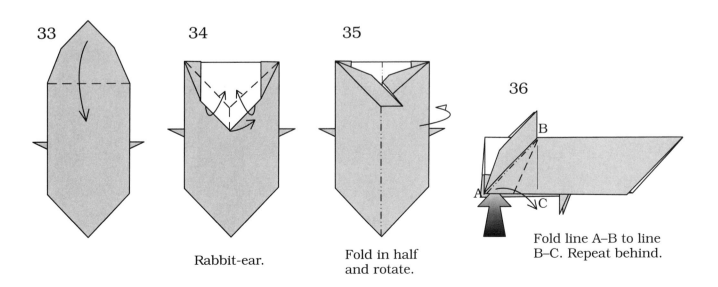

33

34

Rabbit-ear.

35

Fold in half and rotate.

36

B

A

C

Fold line A–B to line B–C. Repeat behind.

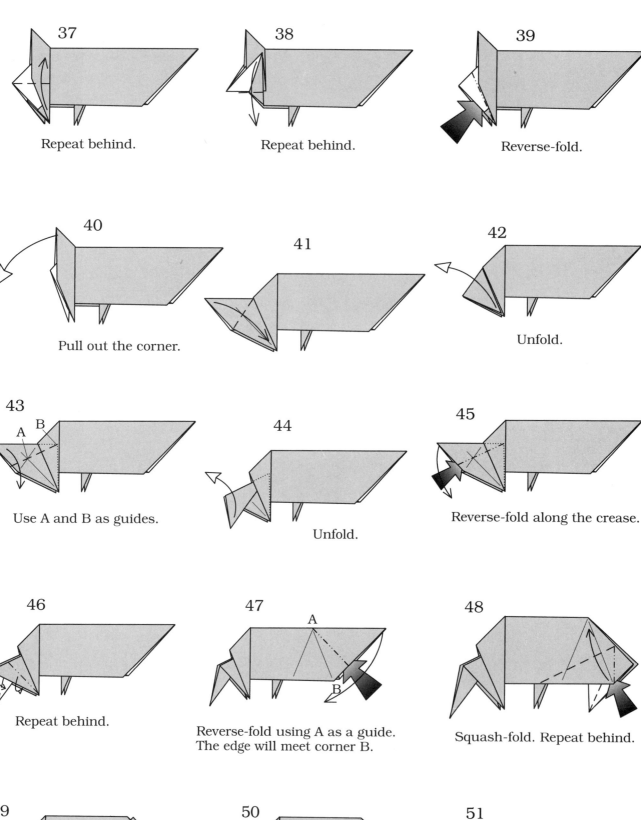

37

Repeat behind.

38

Repeat behind.

39

Reverse-fold.

40

Pull out the corner.

41

42

Unfold.

43

A B

Use A and B as guides.

44

Unfold.

45

Reverse-fold along the crease.

46

Repeat behind.

47

A

B

Reverse-fold using A as a guide.
The edge will meet corner B.

48

Squash-fold. Repeat behind.

49

Repeat behind.

50

51

Do not crease at the head.

90 *African Animals in Origami*

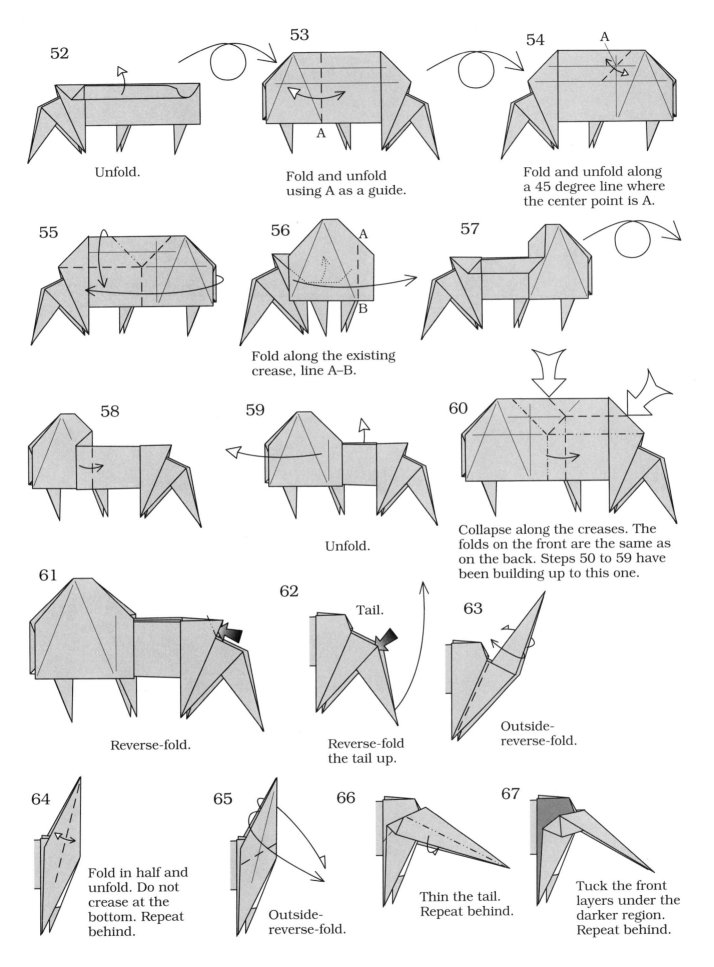

52

Unfold.

53

Fold and unfold using A as a guide.

A

54

A

Fold and unfold along a 45 degree line where the center point is A.

55

56

A

B

Fold along the existing crease, line A–B.

57

58

59

Unfold.

60

Collapse along the creases. The folds on the front are the same as on the back. Steps 50 to 59 have been building up to this one.

61

Reverse-fold.

62

Tail.

Reverse-fold the tail up.

63

Outside-reverse-fold.

64

Fold in half and unfold. Do not crease at the bottom. Repeat behind.

65

Outside-reverse-fold.

66

Thin the tail. Repeat behind.

67

Tuck the front layers under the darker region. Repeat behind.

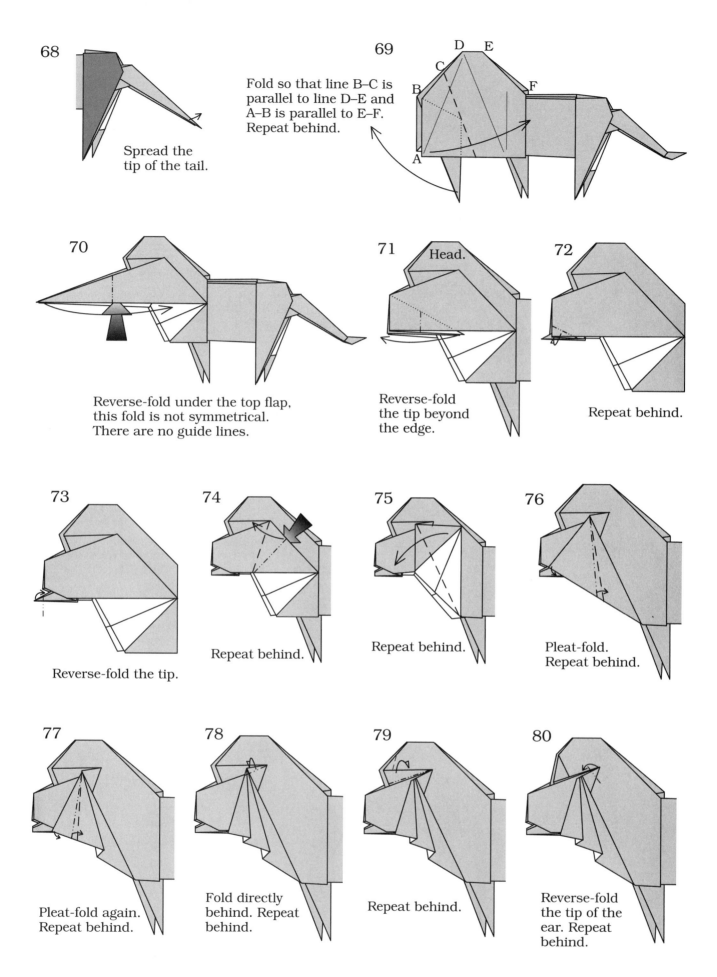

68

Spread the tip of the tail.

69

Fold so that line B–C is parallel to line D–E and A–B is parallel to E–F. Repeat behind.

70

Reverse-fold under the top flap, this fold is not symmetrical. There are no guide lines.

71

Head.

Reverse-fold the tip beyond the edge.

72

Repeat behind.

73

Reverse-fold the tip.

74

Repeat behind.

75

Repeat behind.

76

Pleat-fold. Repeat behind.

77

Pleat-fold again. Repeat behind.

78

Fold directly behind. Repeat behind.

79

Repeat behind.

80

Reverse-fold the tip of the ear. Repeat behind.

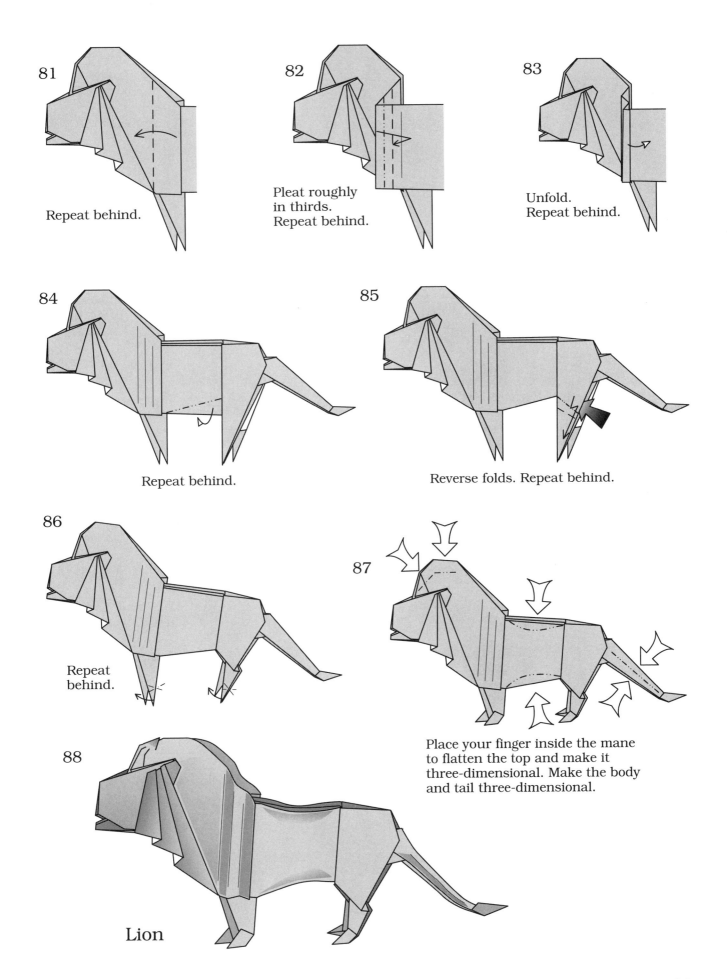

81

Repeat behind.

82

Pleat roughly
in thirds.
Repeat behind.

83

Unfold.
Repeat behind.

84

Repeat behind.

85

Reverse folds. Repeat behind.

86

Repeat
behind.

87

Place your finger inside the mane
to flatten the top and make it
three-dimensional. Make the body
and tail three-dimensional.

88

Lion

Zebra

This model was inspired by my friend, Fumiaki Kawahata San.

The zebra is one of the most well-recognized and highly regarded of all African mammals. The purpose of the characteristic stripes is unknown, although scientists speculate that they may be some form of camouflage. The three living species can be distinguished by subtle differences in their stripe patterns. A fourth species, the quagga, was striped only on the front half of its body. Quaggas were hunted to extinction in the 19th century.

Native zebras are found only in Africa, although some endangered species are being bred elsewhere. Most zebras live in the plains, though some are found in rough mountains. Zebras typically live in small bands, each led by a stallion. They are aggressive fighters and can kill a lion with one blow of a hoof. Zebras are so difficult to train that a movie director who needed a shot of an actress riding a zebra had to settle for putting her on a horse painted with stripes.

1

Fold and unfold along the diagonals.

2

Fold the corners to the center.

3

4

Fold and unfold along the diagonals.

5

6

7

Unfold.

8

Fold and unfold.

9

Use A and B as guides.

A

B

10

11

12

Unfold.

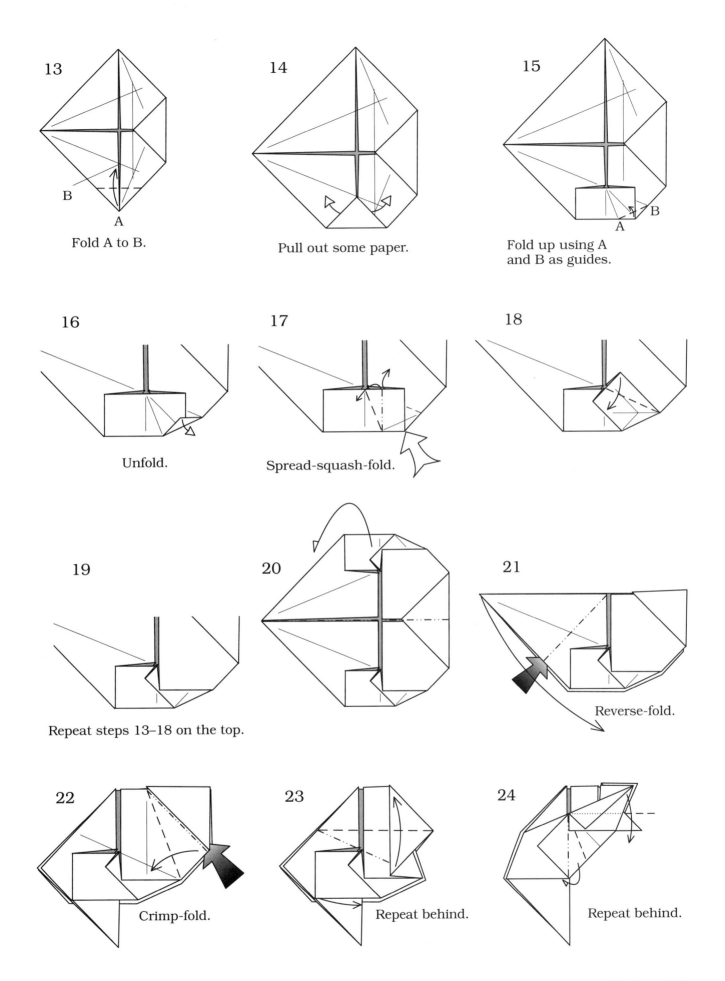

13

B

A

Fold A to B.

14

Pull out some paper.

15

B

A

Fold up using A
and B as guides.

16

Unfold.

17

Spread-squash-fold.

18

19

Repeat steps 13–18 on the top.

20

21

Reverse-fold.

22

Crimp-fold.

23

Repeat behind.

24

Repeat behind.

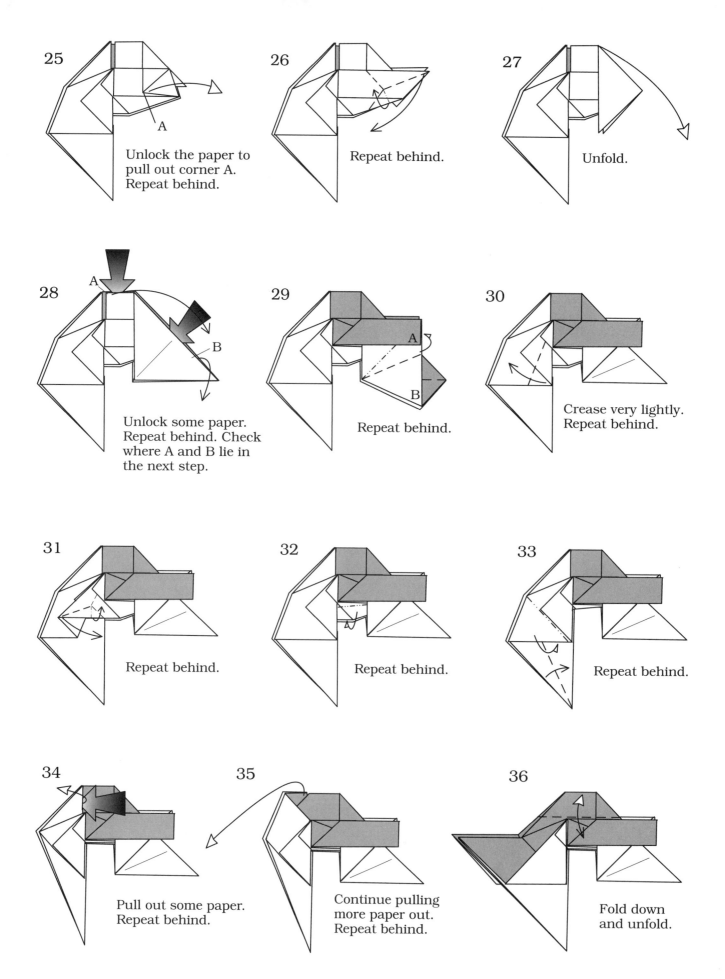

25 Unlock the paper to pull out corner A. Repeat behind.

26 Repeat behind.

27 Unfold.

28 Unlock some paper. Repeat behind. Check where A and B lie in the next step.

29 Repeat behind.

30 Crease very lightly. Repeat behind.

31 Repeat behind.

32 Repeat behind.

33 Repeat behind.

34 Pull out some paper. Repeat behind.

35 Continue pulling more paper out. Repeat behind.

36 Fold down and unfold.

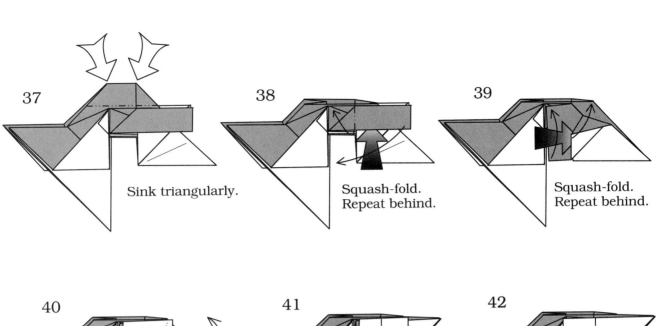

37 Sink triangularly.

38 Squash-fold. Repeat behind.

39 Squash-fold. Repeat behind.

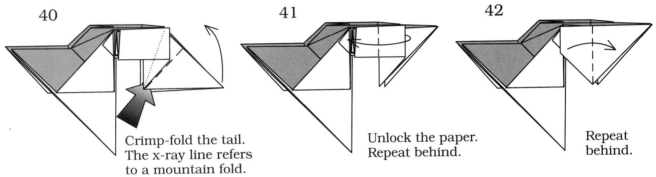

40 Crimp-fold the tail. The x-ray line refers to a mountain fold.

41 Unlock the paper. Repeat behind.

42 Repeat behind.

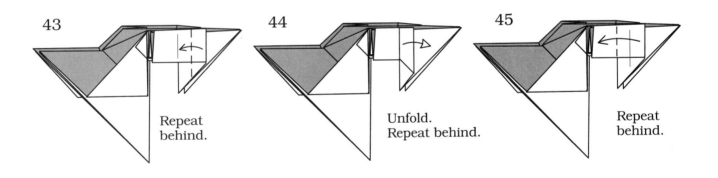

43 Repeat behind.

44 Unfold. Repeat behind.

45 Repeat behind.

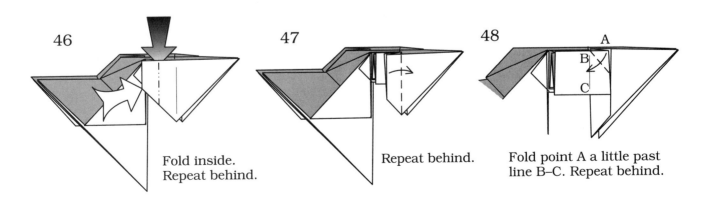

46 Fold inside. Repeat behind.

47 Repeat behind.

48 Fold point A a little past line B–C. Repeat behind.

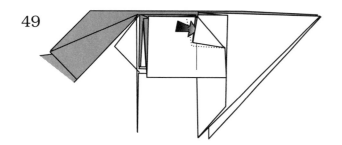

49

Spread apart to the dotted lines
to form a thin, triangular stripe.
Repeat behind.

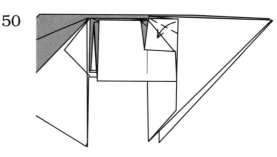

50

Repeat behind.

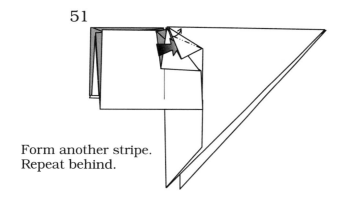

51

Form another stripe.
Repeat behind.

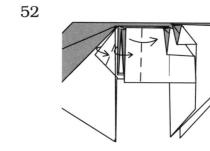

52

Fold all these layers. Stagger
them to form three more
stripes. Repeat behind.

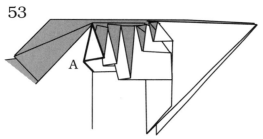

53

A

Tuck the left side of the
bold triangle under
region A. Repeat behind.

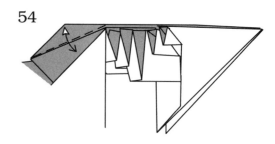

54

Fold down and unfold.
Repeat behind.

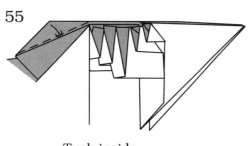

55

Tuck inside.
Repeat behind.

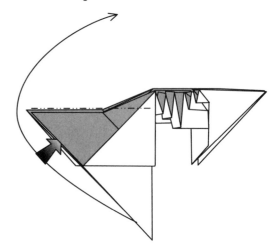

56

Reverse-fold up.

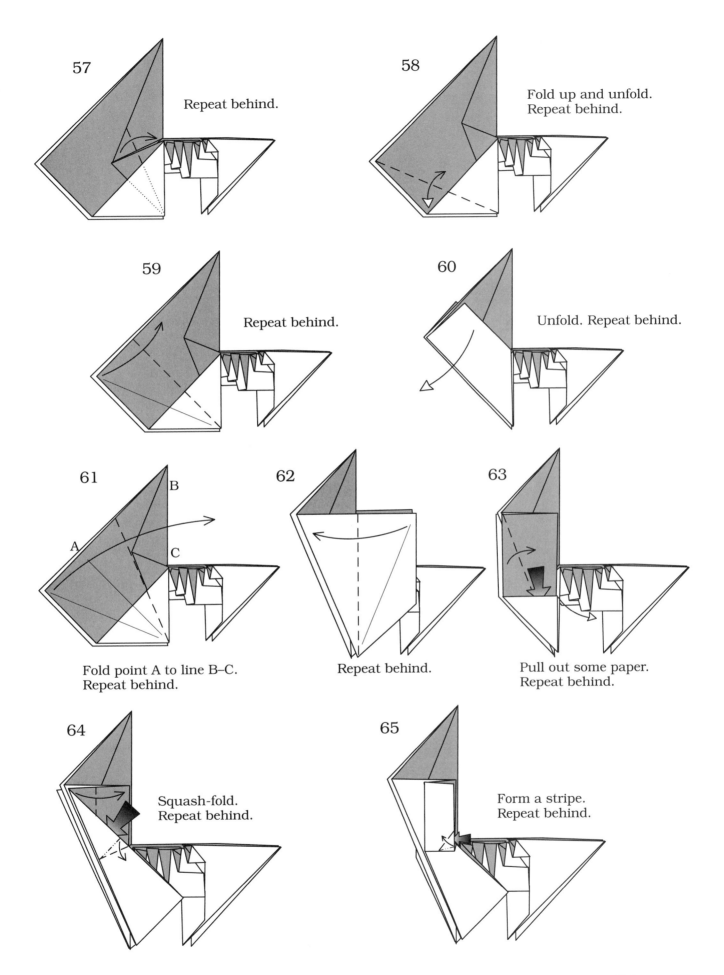

57 Repeat behind.

58 Fold up and unfold.
Repeat behind.

59 Repeat behind.

60 Unfold. Repeat behind.

61 Fold point A to line B–C.
Repeat behind.

62 Repeat behind.

63 Pull out some paper.
Repeat behind.

64 Squash-fold.
Repeat behind.

65 Form a stripe.
Repeat behind.

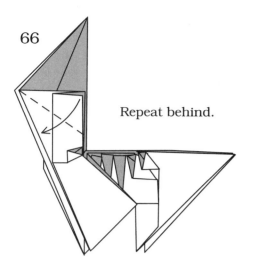

66

Repeat behind.

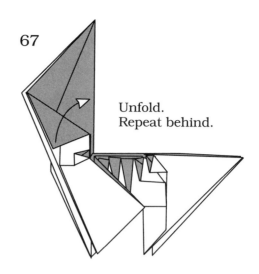

67

Unfold.
Repeat behind.

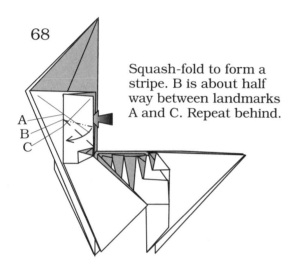

68

Squash-fold to form a
stripe. B is about half
way between landmarks
A and C. Repeat behind.

A
B
C

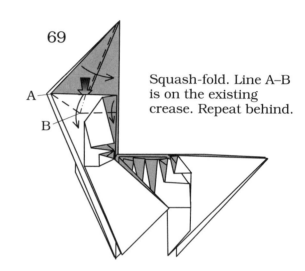

69

Squash-fold. Line A–B
is on the existing
crease. Repeat behind.

A

B

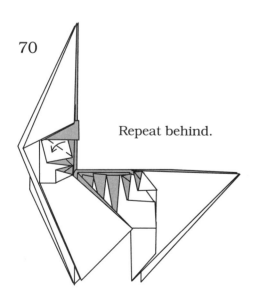

70

Repeat behind.

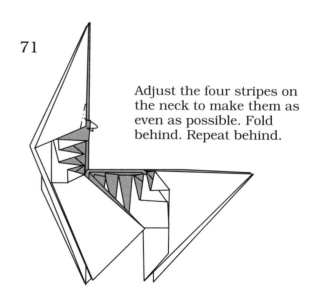

71

Adjust the four stripes on
the neck to make them as
even as possible. Fold
behind. Repeat behind.

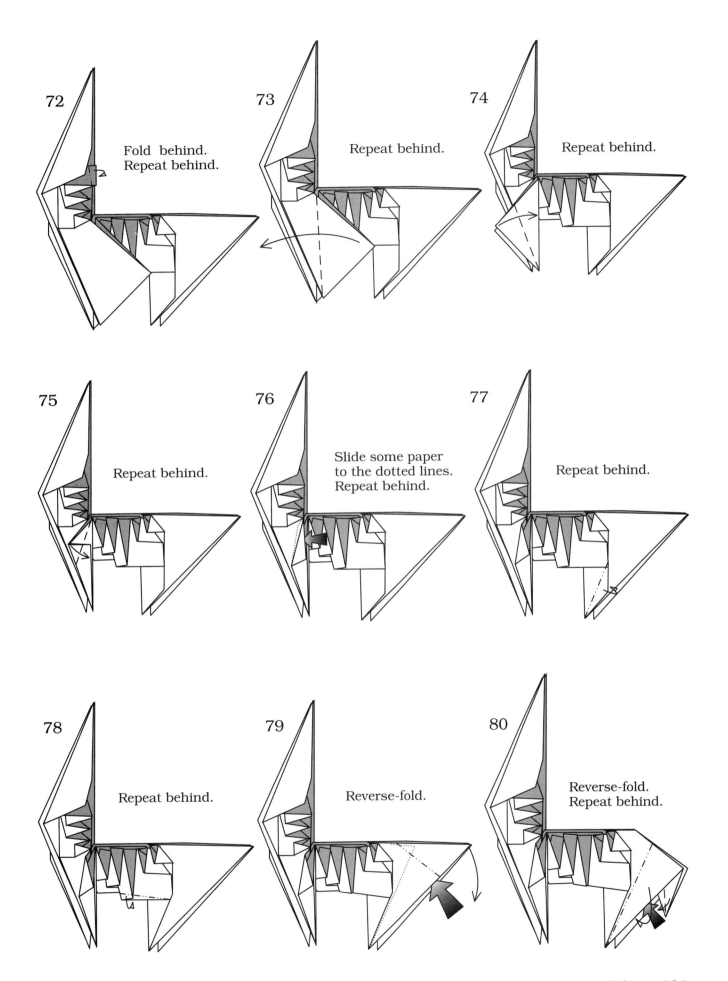

72 Fold behind.
Repeat behind.

73 Repeat behind.

74 Repeat behind.

75 Repeat behind.

76 Slide some paper
to the dotted lines.
Repeat behind.

77 Repeat behind.

78 Repeat behind.

79 Reverse-fold.

80 Reverse-fold.
Repeat behind.

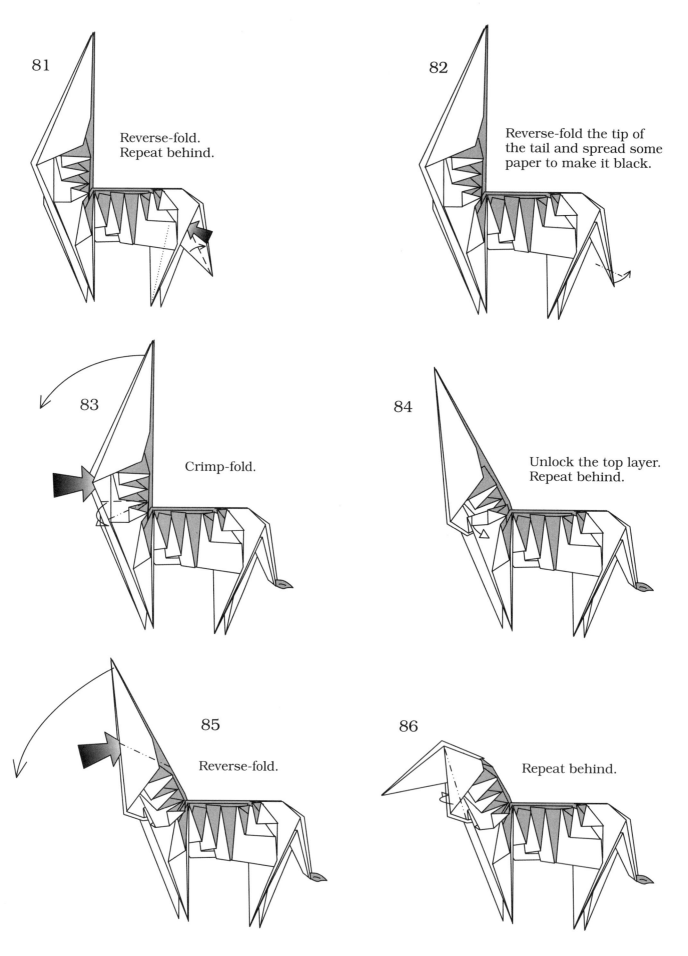

81

Reverse-fold.
Repeat behind.

82

Reverse-fold the tip of
the tail and spread some
paper to make it black.

83

Crimp-fold.

84

Unlock the top layer.
Repeat behind.

85

Reverse-fold.

86

Repeat behind.

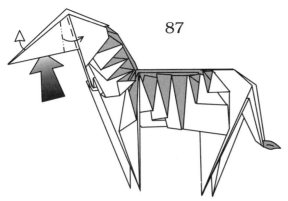

87

Form the ears and shape the head by pulling some paper out. This fold is similar to a crimp fold. Repeat behind at the same time.

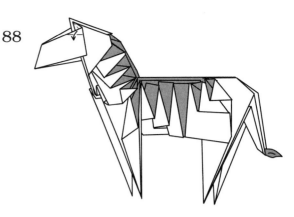

88

Shape the ear. Repeat behind.

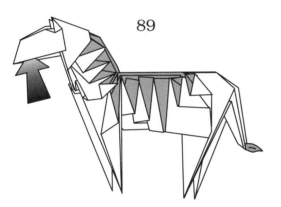

89

Open the front of the head.

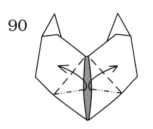

90

Front view of head. Squash folds.

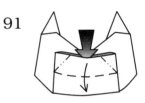

91

Spread-squash-fold.

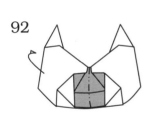

92

Flatten the head.

93

Note: Do not double-rabbit-ear the legs.

Fold the legs in half. They will become thinner and three-dimensional. Fold the hind legs toward the right. Repeat behind.

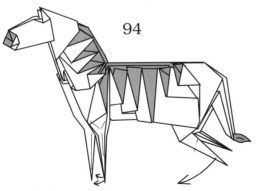

94

Fold the hind legs down. Spread the paper at the bottom of the feet to form hooves. Repeat behind.

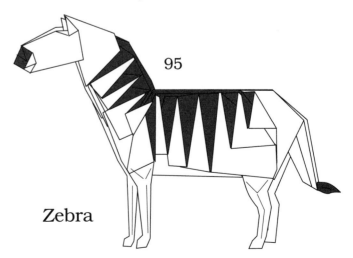

95

Zebra

Giraffe

The giraffe is the tallest animal. Adult males may reach nearly 18 feet in height—5 feet taller than the African elephant. The giraffe's legs can be 8 feet long and the neck may be even longer. Even so, an adult male giraffe's weight of only about 2,000 pounds is only a sixth that of an elephant.

Giraffes inhabit the grasslands or savannas south of the Sahara desert. They feed on leaves, twigs, and fruit of the scattered trees in this region. Like cows, giraffes chew a cud, food that has entered the stomach but is returned to the mouth for further chewing.

Giraffes walk by moving both legs on one side and then both legs on the other side, a movement called pacing. When they gallop, they swing both hind legs out together and throw them in front of the front feet. They may achieve speeds of up to 30 miles per hour.

A giraffe will usually sleep standing up, and when it does lie down, it holds its neck upright or rests its hip on a low tree limb. A giraffe attacks its enemies, chiefly the lion, from standing by kicking with its feet.

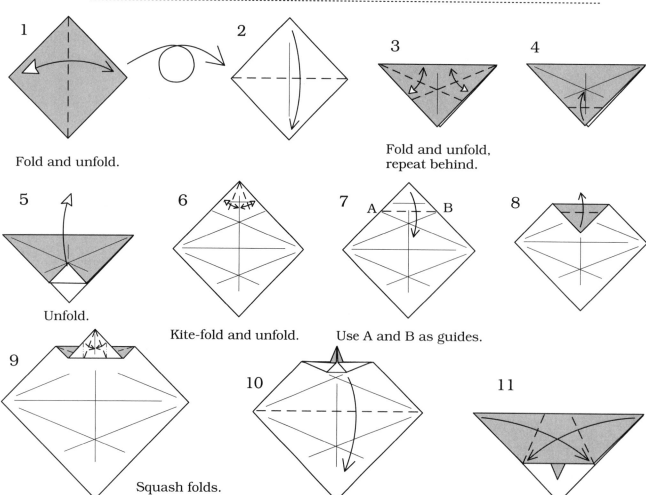

1 Fold and unfold.

2

3 4 Fold and unfold, repeat behind.

5 Unfold.

6 Kite-fold and unfold.

7 A B Use A and B as guides.

8

9 Squash folds.

10

11

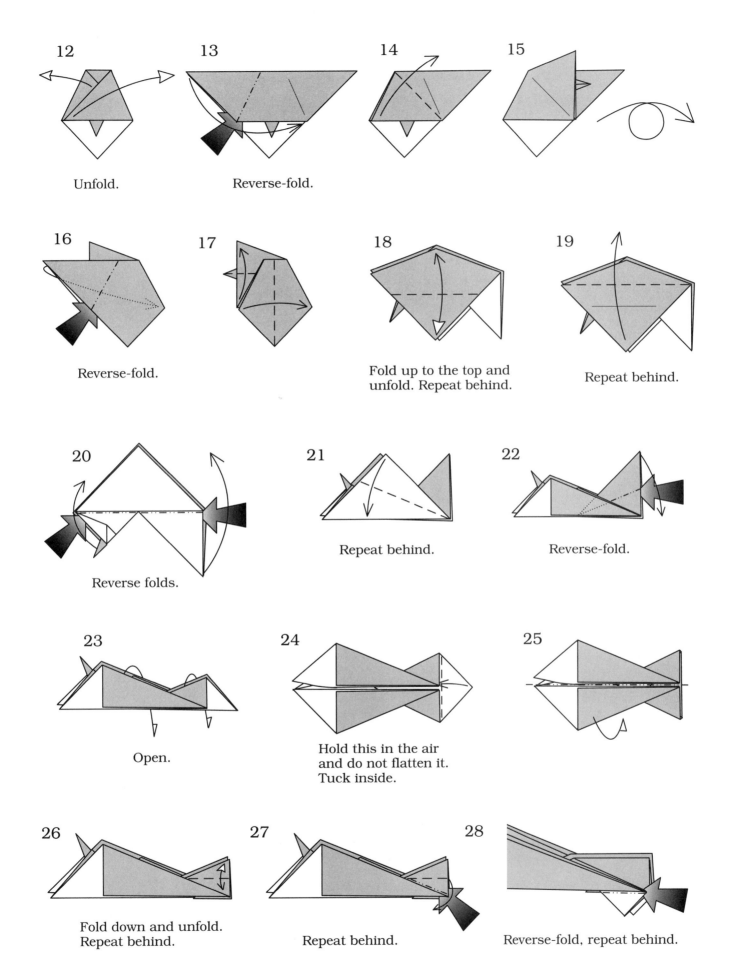

12 Unfold.

13 Reverse-fold.

14

15

16 Reverse-fold.

17

18 Fold up to the top and unfold. Repeat behind.

19 Repeat behind.

20 Reverse folds.

21 Repeat behind.

22 Reverse-fold.

23 Open.

24 Hold this in the air and do not flatten it. Tuck inside.

25

26 Fold down and unfold. Repeat behind.

27 Repeat behind.

28 Reverse-fold, repeat behind.

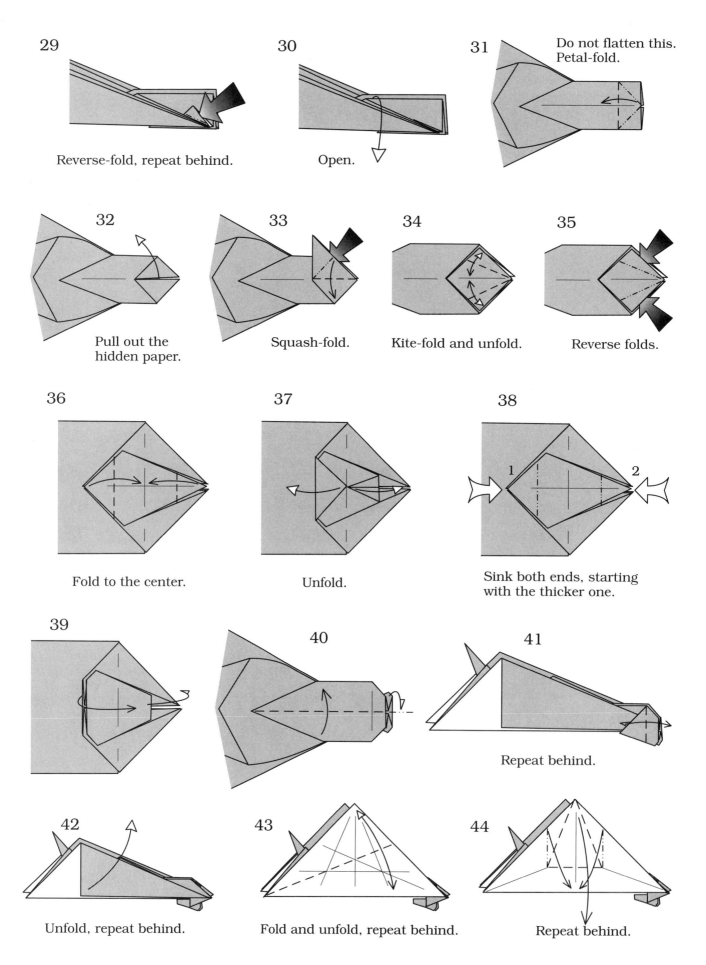

29 Reverse-fold, repeat behind.

30 Open.

31 Do not flatten this. Petal-fold.

32 Pull out the hidden paper.

33 Squash-fold.

34 Kite-fold and unfold.

35 Reverse folds.

36 Fold to the center.

37 Unfold.

38 Sink both ends, starting with the thicker one.

39

40

41 Repeat behind.

42 Unfold, repeat behind.

43 Fold and unfold, repeat behind.

44 Repeat behind.

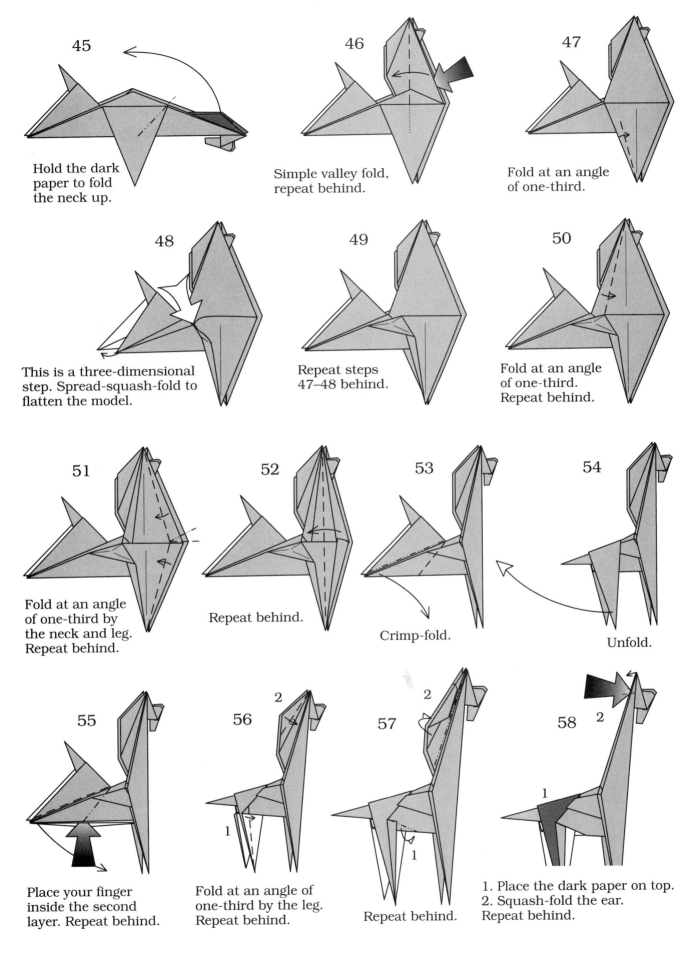

45

Hold the dark paper to fold the neck up.

46

Simple valley fold, repeat behind.

47

Fold at an angle of one-third.

48

This is a three-dimensional step. Spread-squash-fold to flatten the model.

49

Repeat steps 47–48 behind.

50

Fold at an angle of one-third. Repeat behind.

51

Fold at an angle of one-third by the neck and leg. Repeat behind.

52

Repeat behind.

53

Crimp-fold.

54

Unfold.

55

Place your finger inside the second layer. Repeat behind.

56

Fold at an angle of one-third by the leg. Repeat behind.

57

Repeat behind.

58

1. Place the dark paper on top.
2. Squash-fold the ear. Repeat behind.

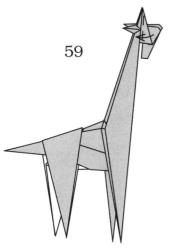

59

Repeat behind.

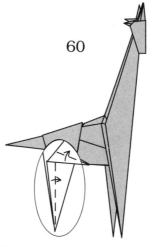

60

The lower hind leg is shown.
Thin at an angle of one-third.
Repeat on the other hind leg.

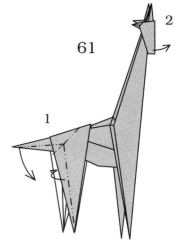

61

1. Fold the tail in half while
   thinning the hind legs at
   an angle of one-third.
2. Slide the head up.

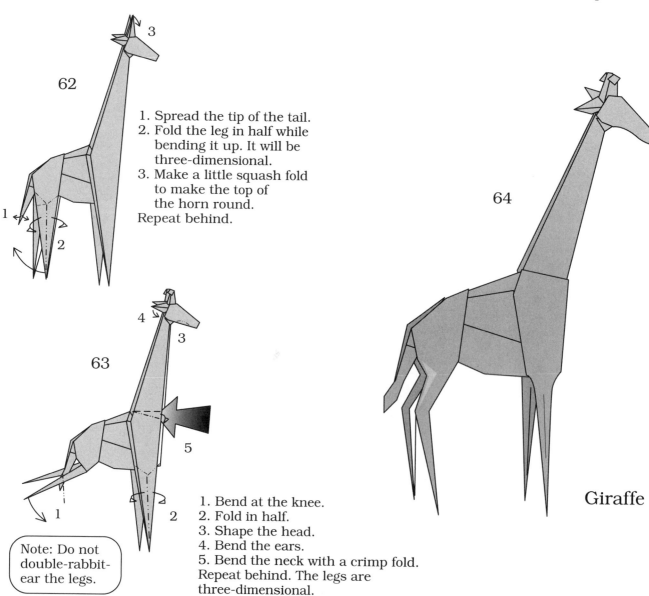

62

1. Spread the tip of the tail.
2. Fold the leg in half while
   bending it up. It will be
   three-dimensional.
3. Make a little squash fold
   to make the top of
   the horn round.
Repeat behind.

63

Note: Do not
double-rabbit-
ear the legs.

1. Bend at the knee.
2. Fold in half.
3. Shape the head.
4. Bend the ears.
5. Bend the neck with a crimp fold.
Repeat behind. The legs are
three-dimensional.

64

Giraffe

Spotted Giraffe

The giraffe is immediately recognized by its patchlike markings or "spots" which vary in color from tawny (light brownish-yellow) to chestnut brown. The lines that separate these patches are lighter tawny or white. This color pattern serves as protection for the giraffe by making it hard to see when standing in the shade of trees. There are different kinds of giraffes distinguished by differences in coat pattern, richness of coloring, and width of the lines. The two primary divisions of giraffes are normal giraffes and reticulated giraffes. Both exhibit spots of brownish color. However, the spots on the reticulated giraffe are larger, darker, and stand out more clearly on a background of white skin. This pattern makes the reticulated giraffe more conspicuous in open fields but harder to see among bushes and trees.

1

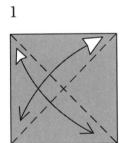

Fold and unfold along the diagonals.

2

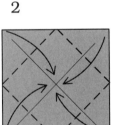

Fold the corners to the center.

3

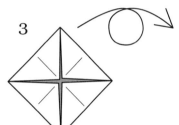

4

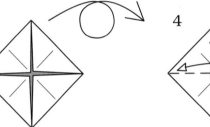

Fold and unfold along the diagonals.

5

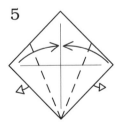

6

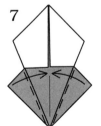

7

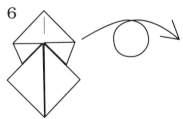

8

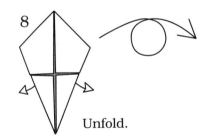

Unfold.

9

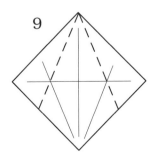

Repeat steps 5–8.

10

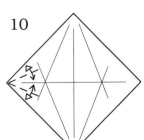

Fold and unfold.

11

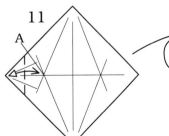

A

Fold and unfold to A.

12

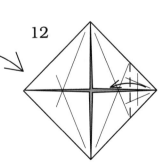

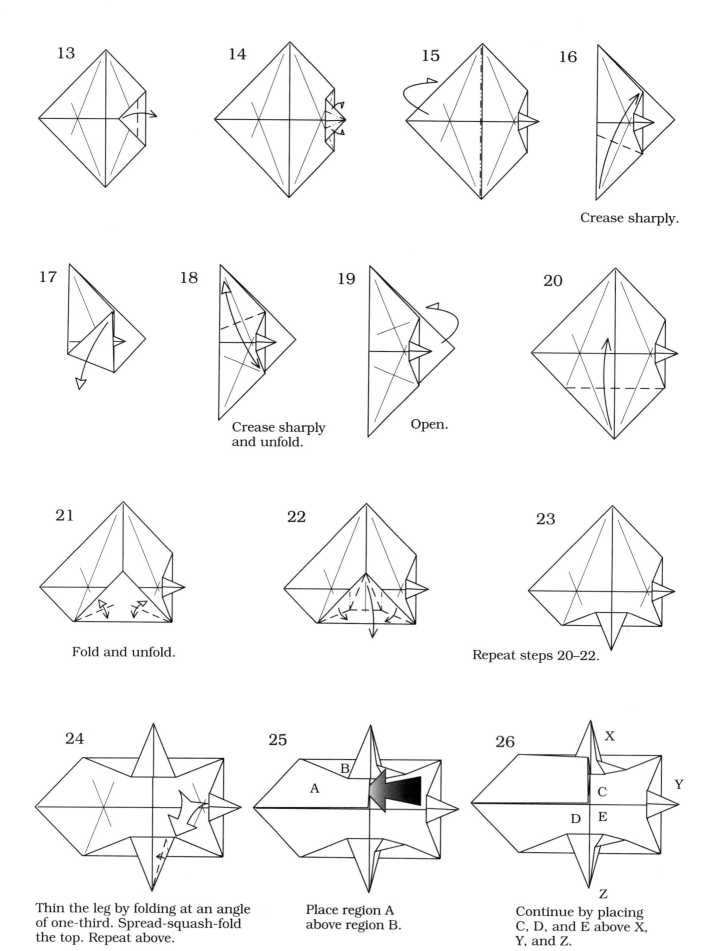

13

14

15

16

Crease sharply.

17

18

Crease sharply
and unfold.

19

Open.

20

21

Fold and unfold.

22

23

Repeat steps 20–22.

24

Thin the leg by folding at an angle
of one-third. Spread-squash-fold
the top. Repeat above.

25

Place region A
above region B.

26

Continue by placing
C, D, and E above X,
Y, and Z.

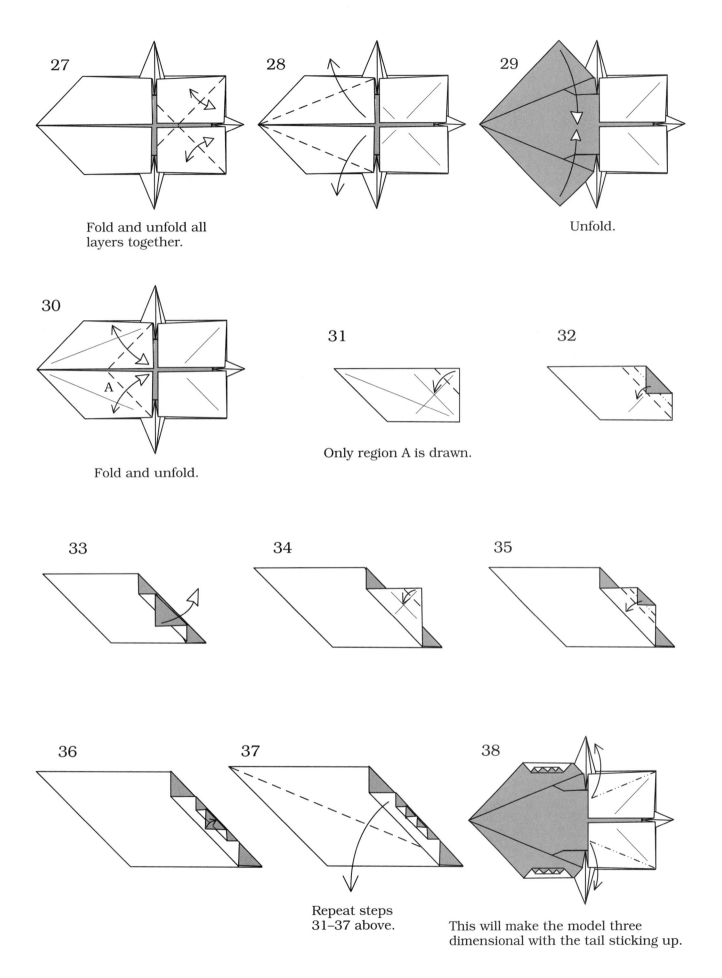

27

Fold and unfold all layers together.

28

29

Unfold.

30

Fold and unfold.

31

Only region A is drawn.

32

33

34

35

36

37

Repeat steps 31–37 above.

38

This will make the model three dimensional with the tail sticking up.

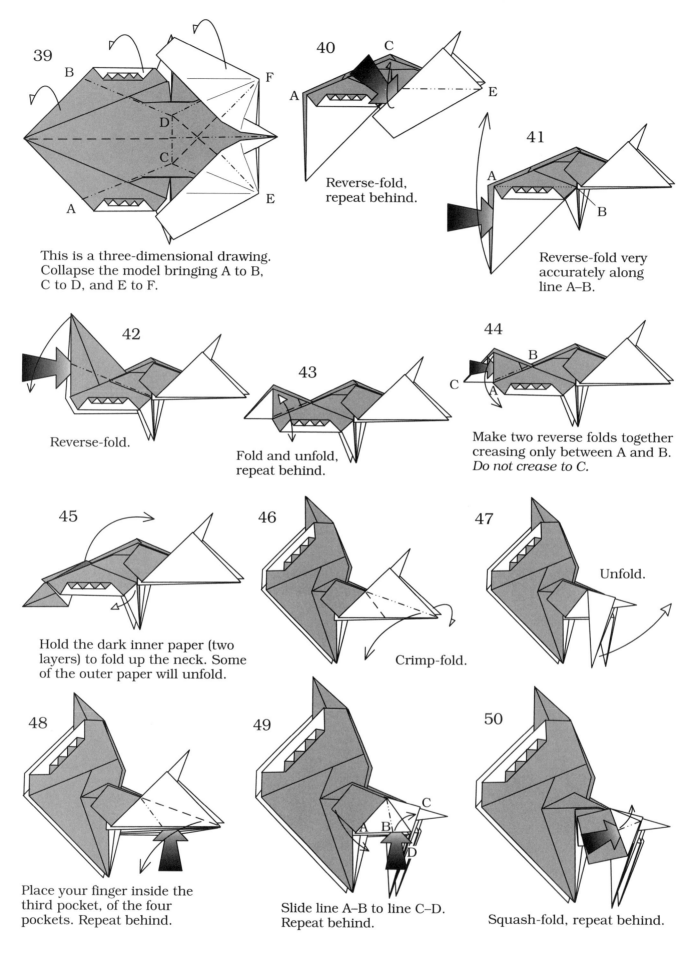

39

B

D

C

A

F

E

This is a three-dimensional drawing. Collapse the model bringing A to B, C to D, and E to F.

40

C

A

C

E

Reverse-fold, repeat behind.

41

A

B

Reverse-fold very accurately along line A–B.

42

Reverse-fold.

43

Fold and unfold, repeat behind.

44

B

C

A

Make two reverse folds together creasing only between A and B. *Do not crease to C.*

45

Hold the dark inner paper (two layers) to fold up the neck. Some of the outer paper will unfold.

46

Crimp-fold.

47

Unfold.

48

Place your finger inside the third pocket, of the four pockets. Repeat behind.

49

A   B   C

D

Slide line A–B to line C–D. Repeat behind.

50

Squash-fold, repeat behind.

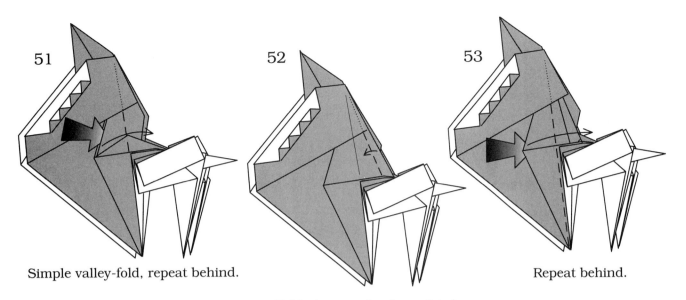

51 Simple valley-fold, repeat behind.

52 Fold at an angle of one-third, repeat behind.

53 Repeat behind.

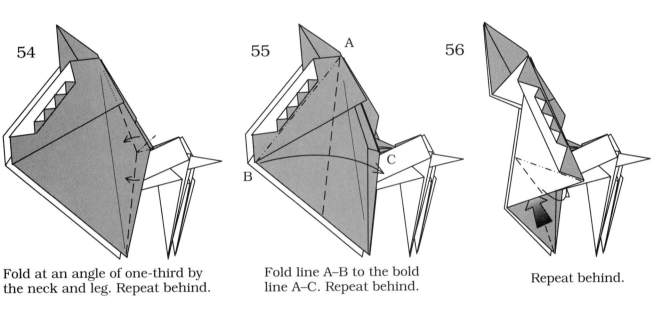

54 Fold at an angle of one-third by the neck and leg. Repeat behind.

55 Fold line A–B to the bold line A–C. Repeat behind.

56 Repeat behind.

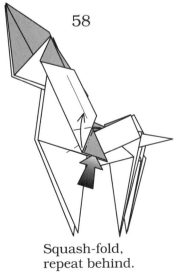

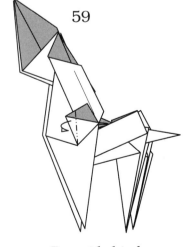

57 Repeat behind.

58 Squash-fold, repeat behind.

59 Repeat behind.

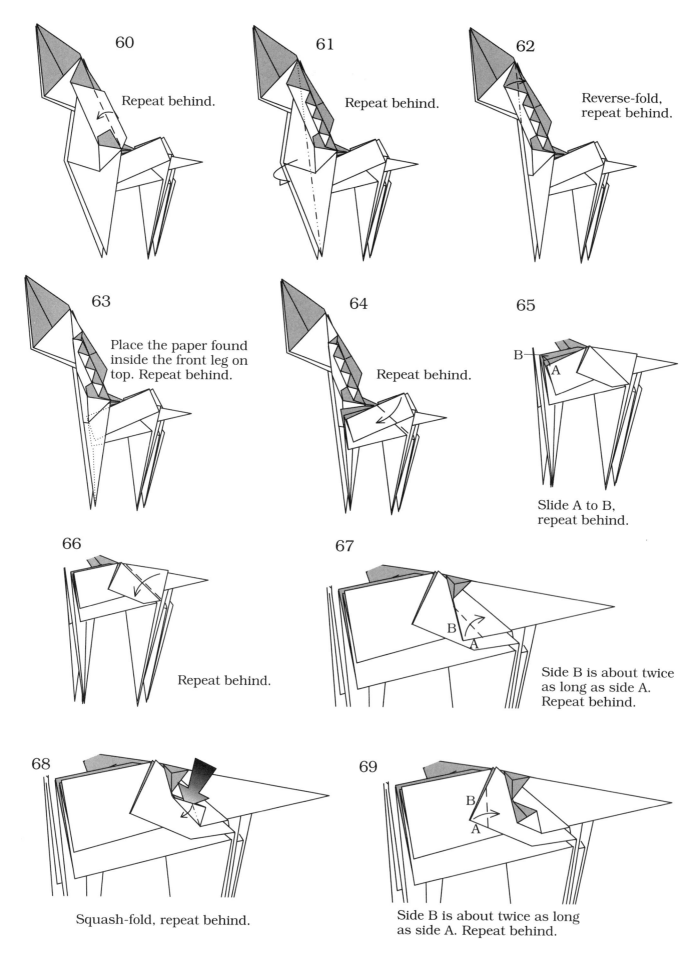

60 Repeat behind.

61 Repeat behind.

62 Reverse-fold, repeat behind.

63 Place the paper found inside the front leg on top. Repeat behind.

64 Repeat behind.

65 B — A
Slide A to B, repeat behind.

66 Repeat behind.

67 B A
Side B is about twice as long as side A. Repeat behind.

68 Squash-fold, repeat behind.

69 B A
Side B is about twice as long as side A. Repeat behind.

70

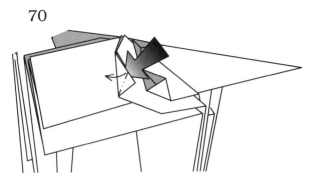

Squash-fold, repeat behind.

71

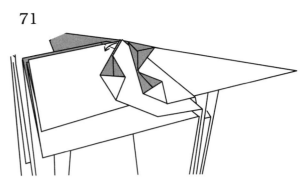

Reverse-fold, repeat behind.

72

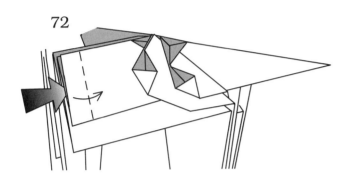

Squash-fold, repeat behind.

73

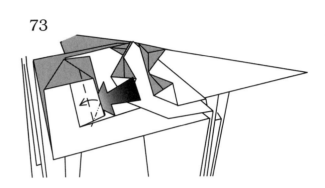

Squash-fold, repeat behind.

74

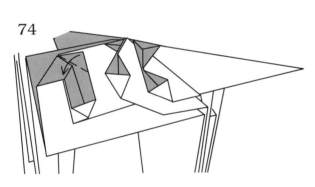

Repeat behind.

75

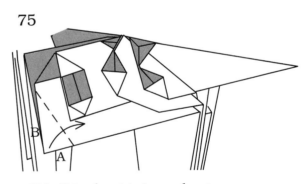

Side B is about twice as long
as side A. Repeat behind.

76

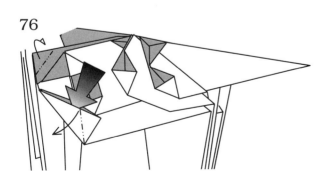

Squash-fold, repeat behind.

77

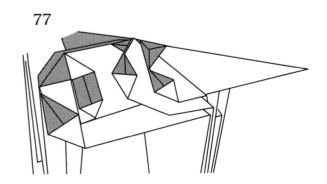

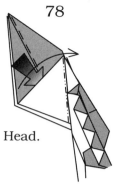

78

Head.

Reverse-fold,
repeat behind.

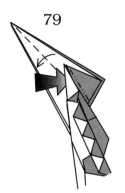

79

Reverse-fold,
repeat behind.

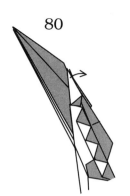

80

Slide out the ear,
repeat behind.

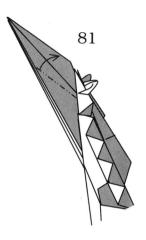

81

Slide the top layer,
repeat behind.

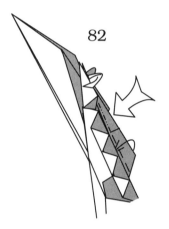

82

Tuck inside,
repeat behind.

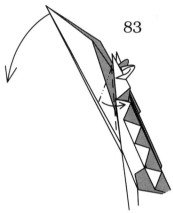

83

Crimp-fold.

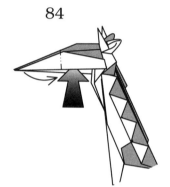

84

Reverse-fold.

85

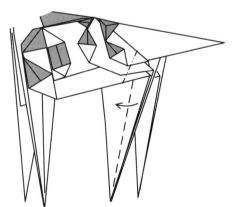

86

Fold the top four layers
together at an angle of
one-third. Repeat behind.

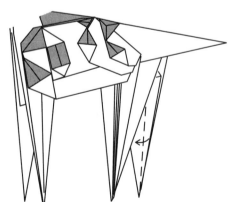

87

Fold the two layers from the
underside together at an
angle of one-third, repeat.

88

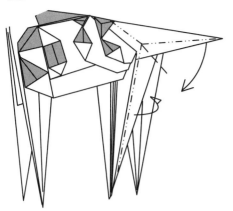

Fold the tail in half while
thinning the hind legs at
an angle of one-third.

89

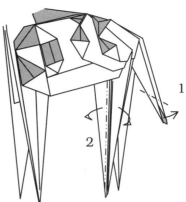

1. Show the colored paper at the tail.
2. Thin the leg in half, repeat behind.

90

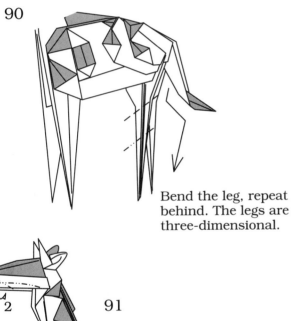

Bend the leg, repeat
behind. The legs are
three-dimensional.

91

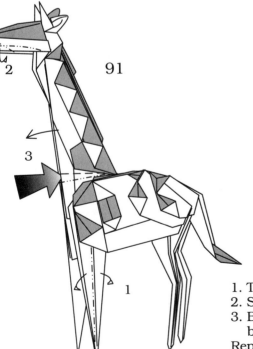

92

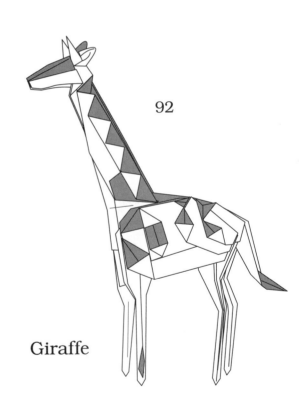

Giraffe

1. Thin the leg and make it three-dimensional.
2. Shape the head.
3. Bend the neck. This is not a real fold,
   but a three-dimensional shaping.
Repeat behind.

Basic Folds

Rabbit Ear.

To fold a rabbit ear, one corner is folded in half and laid down to a side.

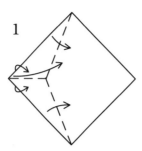 1

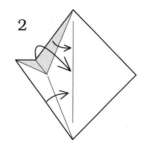 2

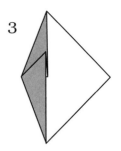 3

Fold a rabbit ear.

A three-dimensional intermediate step.

Double Rabbit Ear.

If you were to bend a straw you would be folding the double rabbit ear.

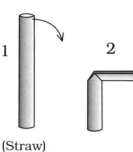

1   2

(Straw)

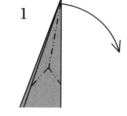 1

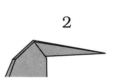 2

Make a double rabbit ear.

Squash Fold.

In a squash fold, some paper is opened and then made flat. The shaded arrow shows where to place your finger.

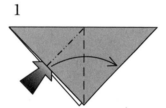 1

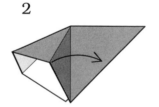 2

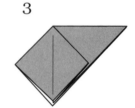 3

Squash-fold.

A three-dimensional intermediate step.

Petal Fold.

In a petal fold, one point is folded up while two opposite sides meet each other.

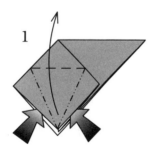 1

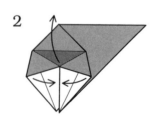 2

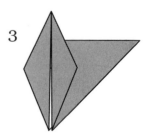 3

Petal-fold.

A three-dimensional intermediate step.